Bagging It with Puppets!

Paper Bag Puppets to Introduce the Alphabet and Letter/Sound Recognition

by Gloria Mehrens and Karen Wick

Fearon Teacher Aids
a division of
David S. Lake Publishers
Belmont, California

Illustrations created by Gloria Mehrens and Karen Wick and redrawn by Duane Bibby

ISBN 0-8224-0677-2

Printed in the United States of America
1. 9 8 7 6 5 4 3 2

Contents

Introduction

Bagging It with Puppets! evolved during our years of working with children in both kindergarten and first grade. To introduce new letter sounds to our students in a fun and creative way, we created a puppet for each vowel and consonant. Excited friends and teachers encouraged us to make a book. Now we are delighted to share these puppets with you.

Your students will develop perceptual and motor skills as they construct each of the puppets in this book. Putting together the puppets can help develop and strengthen:

- listening skills
- ability to follow written and oral directions
- ability to understand sequencing
- awareness of spatial relationships
- eye-hand coordination
- auditory memory
- awareness of shapes, sizes, and colors
- visual discrimination

You can use the puppets in numerous ways throughout the curriculum. We have used them in a "sound of the week" program to enhance reading and phonics instruction and to motivate students. Each week we introduce a new letter/sound and a new puppet.

Some of the objectives developed in the "sound of the week" program involve sound/symbol relationships, vocabulary development, auditory discrimination, rhyming, role-playing, word building, and handwriting. Enrichment activities we have used in this program include the following:

1. *Handwriting* Have the students write both upper- and lower-case letters and words with each initial letter sound.
2. *Brainstorming* Ask children to give all the words they can think of for the given sound of the week. Record each word as it is given on the chalkboard or on chart paper. Proceed until the board is full. Leave the board intact throughout the week so the children can use it for reference.
3. *Sound Books* Using the list of words on the chalkboard (see above), have each child write and illustrate each word on a piece of paper. Staple the pages together on one side to make a small letter/sound book.
4. *Word-Object Table* Set up a table to which students can bring objects that begin with the sound of the week. Label the objects.
5. *Bulletin Board* With the children, create a sound-symbol bulletin board for the week. Students can make their own labeled pictures or cut pictures from magazines.
6. *Stories* Integrate stories that relate to the sound of the week. For the letter *W*, you can use *Whistle for Willie* by Ezra Jack Keats. For the letter *H*, consider *How, Hippo!* by Marcia Brown.
7. *Songs* Look for songs that relate to the sound of the week.
8. *Cooking* Consider making foods that begin with the sound of the week—blueberry muffins for the letter *B*, or ice cream for the letter *I*.
9. *Dramatization* Pantomime or act out words that begin with the sound of the week.
10. *Treasure Hunt* Hide objects or pictures of objects that begin with the sound of the week.
11. *Large Letter* Cut a large letter (12″ × 18″) out of colored construction paper and ask each child to color a picture of an object that begins with that letter. Paste the pictures on the large letter.
12. *Silly Sentences* Use sentences made up of words beginning with the letter of the week. *We have included some of our own on the following page.* The sentences can be used for directed handwriting and for inspiring student-created silly sentences.

The enrichment activity possibilities are endless! Both you and your students can create new ideas each week.

Silly Sentences

Rr Randy Robot's red roadster races rapidly.

Ss Silly Scarecrow scribbles silly stories.

Tt Tanya Tiger tickles Terry Turtle's toes.

Mm Merry Mouse munches marshmallows.

Ff Firefighter Fred fights fires frantically.

Bb Billy Boy bats big blue balls.

Cc Curly Cowboy catches coral-colored cows.

Dd Doctor Donna dunks delicious donuts.

Gg Greta Girl grows green grasshoppers.

Hh Harry Hippopotamus hops home happily.

Jj Jack-in-the-Box jumps joyfully.

Ll Lionel Lion loves lemon lollipops.

Nn Nurse Nancy nibbles nachos.

Kk Kooky Kookaburra kicks kettles.

Pp Peter Pig paints pretty pictures.

Qq Queenie Queen's quarterback quit.

Vv Victor Viking vacuums vans.

Ww Winnie Witch wears weird wigs.

Xx X-Ray Boy examines xylophones.

Yy Yakky Yak yanks yellow yo-yos.

Zz Zeke Zebra zaps zinnias.

Aa Astronaut Annie advertises applesauce.

Ee Ellie Elephant exits elevators elegantly.

Ii Ill Izzy is in intensive care.

Oo Ollie Octopus offers omelettes.

Uu Uncle Sam unpacks umbrellas.

Aa Amy Angel ate angel cake.

Ee Edith Eagle eats enormous eclairs.

Ii Ice-Cream Ike isolates icicles.

Oo Ogie Ogre owns overshoes.

Uu Una Unicorn usually uses uniforms.

Randy Robot

Materials: ☆

- paper lunch bags (11″ × 5¾″) for puppet base
- orange construction paper (body, head)
- yellow construction paper (arms, legs, letter card, teeth, ears, eyes, antenna)
- black construction paper (base for eyes, base for teeth)
- crayons
- scissors
- paste
- paper clips
- paper cutter
- white china marker
- patterns on pages 6–11

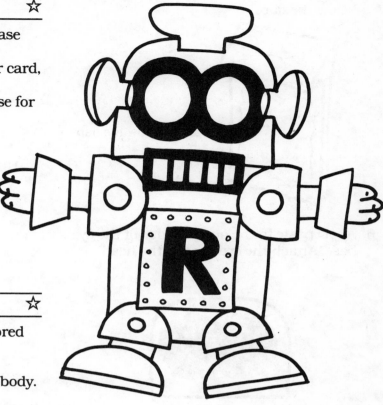

Preparation: ☆

1. Duplicate patterns on the appropriate colored construction paper.
2. Using a paper cutter, cut sheets of orange construction paper 6″ × 9″ for the robot's body. You can cut four to five sheets at a time.
3. With the white china marker, trace the base for eyes and the base for teeth (Pattern E) on black construction paper.
4. For each child, make a packet containing:
   a) Pattern A (teeth, eyes, ears)
   b) Pattern B (antenna, letter card)
   c) Pattern C (arms)
   d) Pattern D (legs)
   e) pretraced Pattern E (base for eyes, base for teeth)
   f) Pattern F (head)
   g) one precut body
   h) one paper lunch bag
   i) one paper clip
   Clip a–g together on the paper bag with the paper clip.

Procedure: ☆

1. Distribute to each student:
   a) paste
   b) crayons
   c) scissors
   d) puppet packet
   Demonstrate the following steps for the students.
2. Unclip the puppet packet and write your name on the back side of the paper lunch bag. Place the bag aside for now.
3. With black crayon, outline the interior and exterior lines on all the robot parts on the duplicated sheets. Color the letter *R* with black crayon.
4. Cut all duplicated patterns along the dotted lines, *being careful not to cut away the crayoned outlines.*

5. With one finger, put paste on the outside edge of the bag *(do not get paste on the flap)*. Place the body on the pasted edge, below the flap.

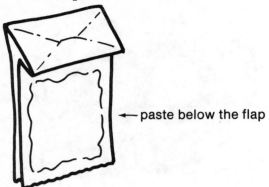

← paste below the flap

6. Apply paste to the outside edge of the eye base. Attach the eye base to the head.

7. Run paste along the outside edge of each eye. Place the eyes on the eye base and smooth down.

8. Run paste along the inside edge of each ear. Attach the ears to each side of the head.

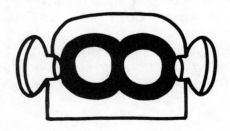

9. Apply paste to the bottom of the antenna. Paste the antenna on top of the head.

10. Run paste along the top edge of the base for teeth. Attach the base to the lower part of the head, beneath the eyes.

11. Apply paste to the back of the teeth and paste them to the teeth base.

12. Apply paste to the outside edge of the bag's flap.

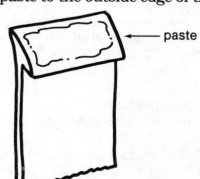

← paste

13. Place the head on the pasted flap and smooth down.

14. Run paste along the inside edge of each arm. Paste the arms on the outside of the body, below the flap of the bag.

15. Run paste along the inside edge of each leg. Paste the legs on the outside of the body, at the bottom edge of the bag.

16. Apply paste to the back side of the letter card. Place the letter card between the arms and legs of the robot.
17. Let the puppet dry before using.

Robot 5

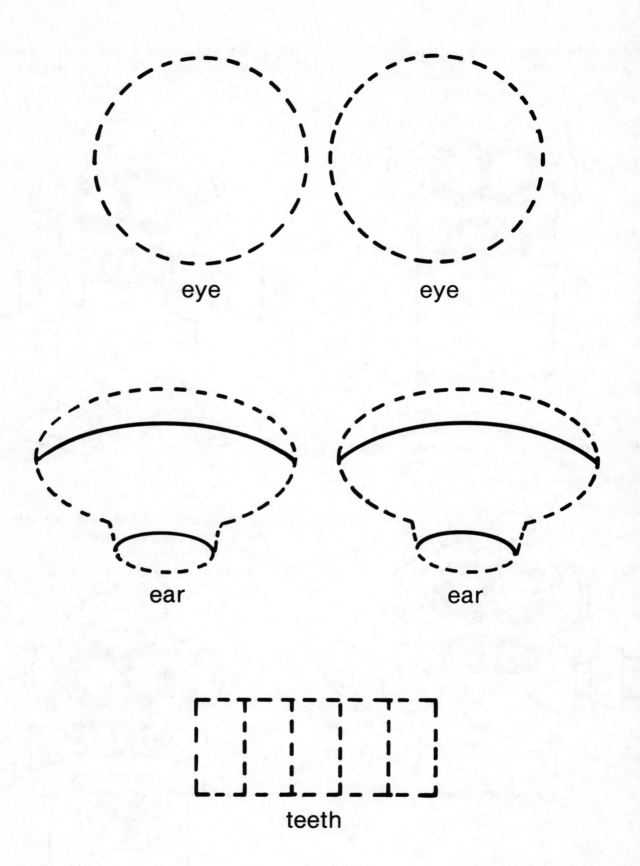

eye eye

ear ear

teeth

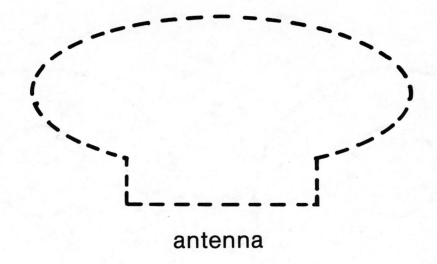

antenna

letter card

Pattern B (yellow)

Robot 7

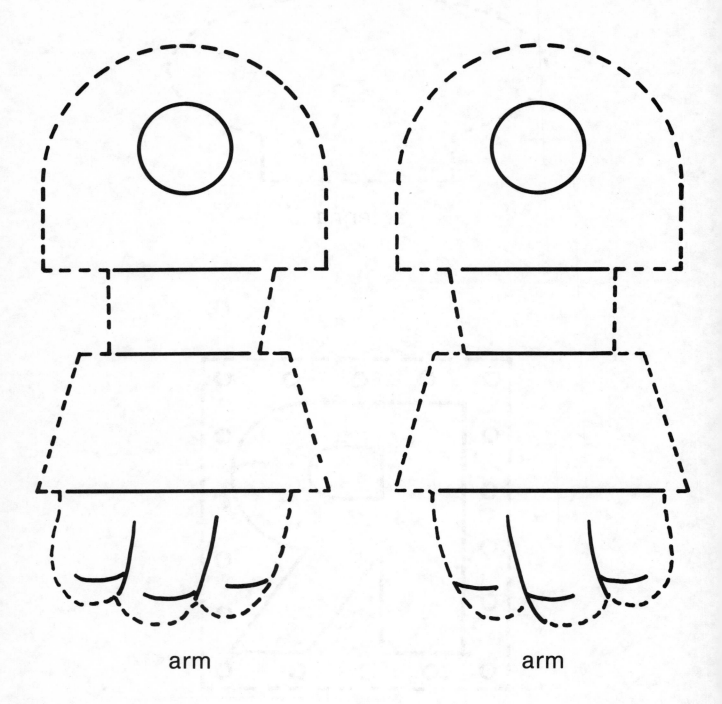

arm

arm

Bagging It with Puppets! © 1988 David S. Lake Publishers

8 Robot

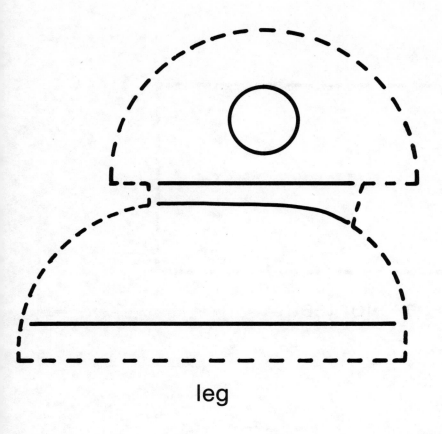

leg

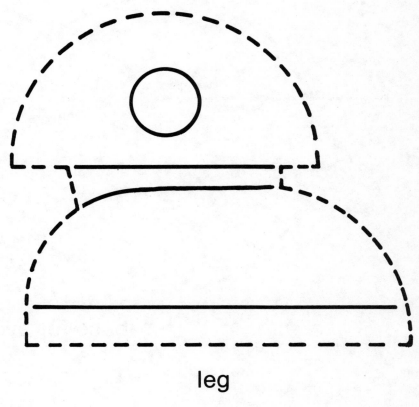

leg

Pattern D (yellow)

Robot 9

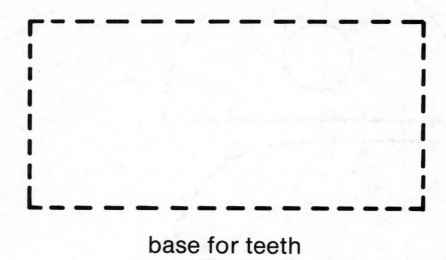

base for teeth

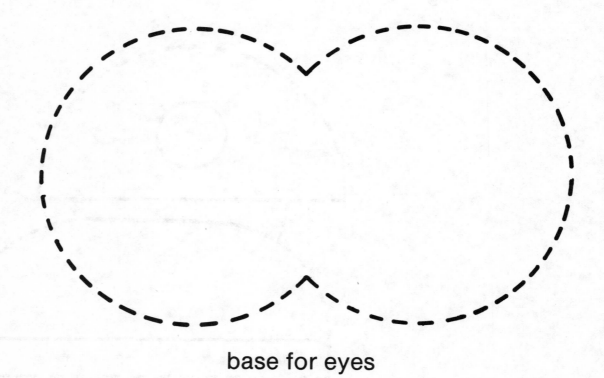

base for eyes

Pattern E (black)

Bagging It with Puppets! © 1988 David S. Lake Publishers

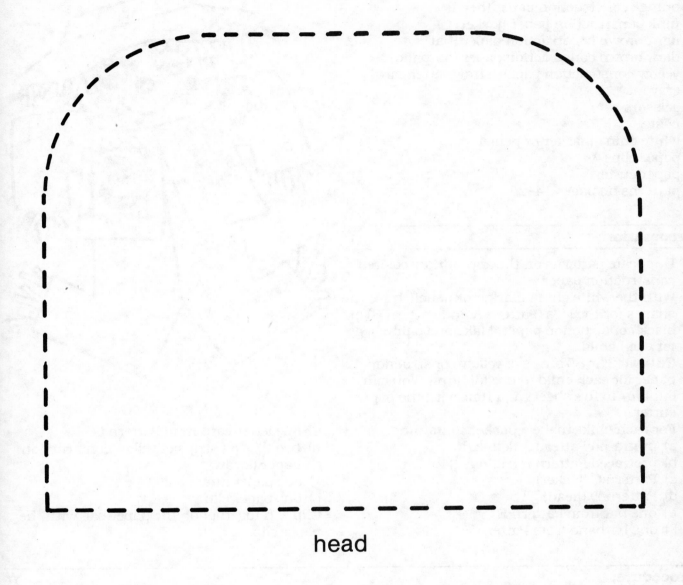

head

Pattern F (orange)

Robot 11

Silly Scarecrow

Materials: ☆

- paper lunch bags (11″ × 5¾″) for puppet base
- black construction paper (legs)
- orange construction paper (head)
- pink construction paper (jacket)
- light brown construction paper (hat)
- dark brown construction paper (hatband)
- yellow construction paper (straw, letter card)
- crayons
- scissors
- paste
- white china marker or pencil
- paper clips
- paper cutter
- patterns on pages 14–20

Preparation: ☆

1. Duplicate patterns on the appropriate colored construction paper.
2. With the white china marker or pencil, trace the shapes for the legs (Pattern A and Pattern B) on black construction paper. Make one pair of legs for each child.
3. Cut two 2″ × 8″ strips of yellow construction paper for each child to use for straw. You can cut four to five sheets at a time with the paper cutter.
4. For each child, make a packet containing:
   a) pretraced Pattern A (left leg)
   b) pretraced Pattern B (right leg)
   c) Pattern C (jacket)
   d) Pattern D (head)
   e) one hat from Pattern E
   f) one hatband from Pattern F
   g) one letter card from Pattern G
   h) two 2″ × 8″ strips of yellow construction paper (straw)
   i) one paper lunch bag
   j) one paper clip
   Clip a–h together on the paper bag with the paper clip.

Procedure: ☆

1. Distribute to each student:
   a) paste
   b) crayons
   c) scissors
   d) puppet packet
   Demonstrate the following steps for the students.
2. Unclip the puppet packet and write your name on the back side of the paper lunch bag. Place the bag aside for now.
3. Cut all duplicated and pretraced patterns along the dotted lines.
4. With one finger, put paste on the outside edge of the bag *(do not get paste on the flap)*. Place the left leg on the left side, and the right leg on the right side of the bag. Smooth down.

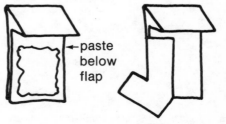

paste below flap

left leg   both legs

5. Paste the letter card on the lower part of the jacket. Color the patches and add patch stitches. Color the letter S with black crayon.

6. Run paste along the top edge of the legs.
7. Place the jacket on the paste and smooth down. Do not get paste on the flap of the bag.

8. Run paste along the hatband. Attach the hatband to the hat. Add # marks to the hat with black crayon.

9. Run paste along the straight edge of the head. Place the hat on the pasted edge and smooth down.

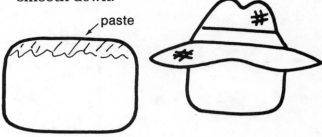

paste

10. With crayons, add the facial features. With white crayon, color two large ovals for the eyes. Outline the eyes with black and add pupils. Add black lashes. Add the nose. With red crayon, add the mouth. With pink crayon, add cheeks.

11. Cut up the two strips of yellow construction paper to make straw. Add the straw under the ends of the arms, legs, and hat.
12. Let the puppet dry before using.

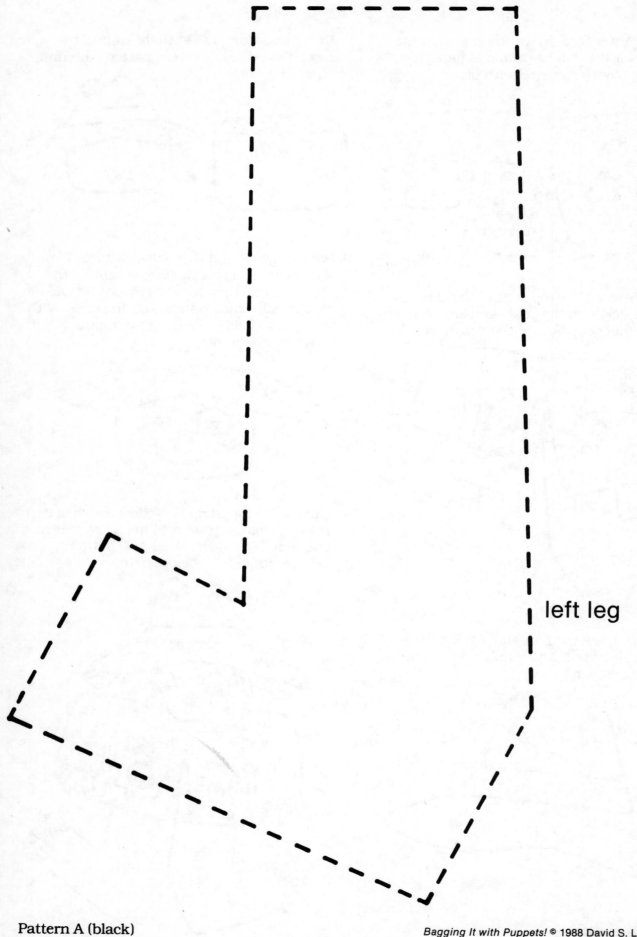

left leg

Pattern A (black)

14 Scarecrow

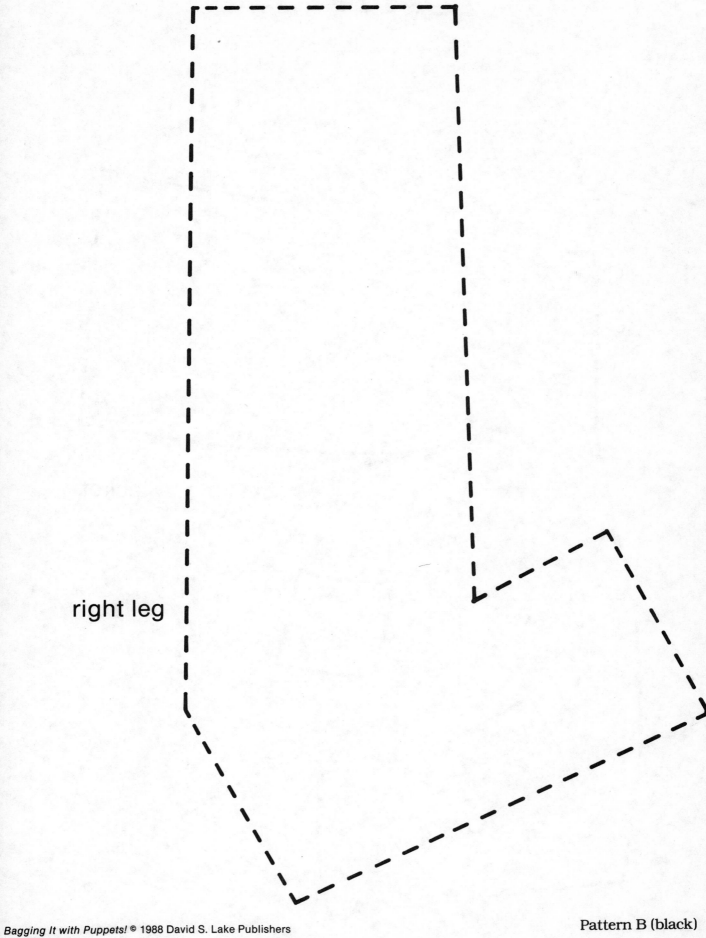

right leg

Pattern B (black)

Scarecrow 15

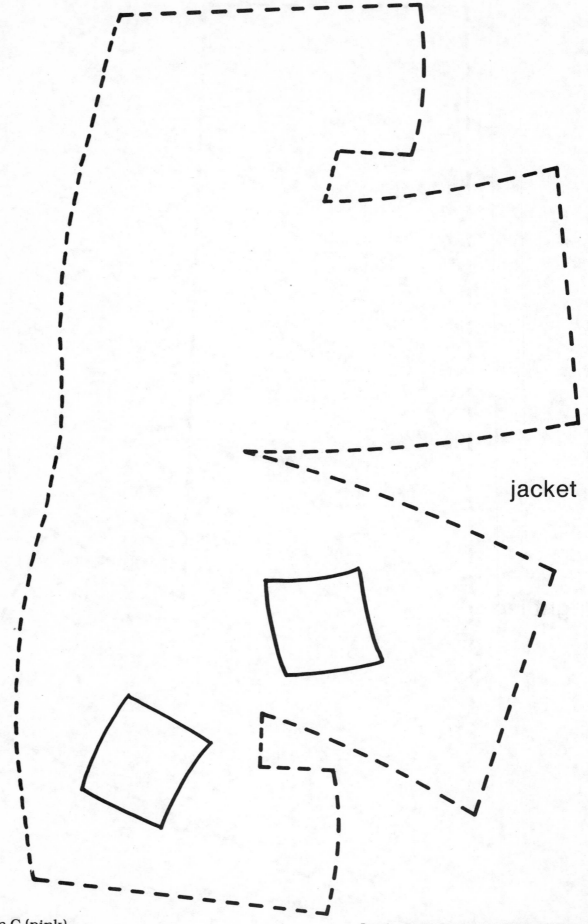

jacket

Pattern C (pink)

16   Scarecrow

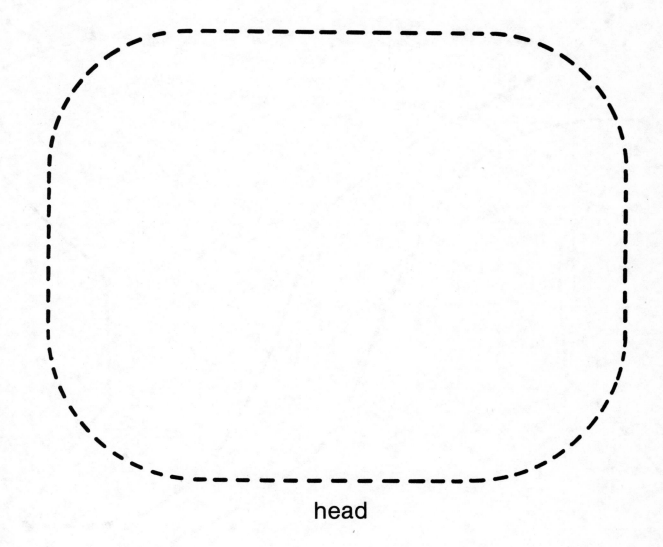

head

Pattern D (orange)

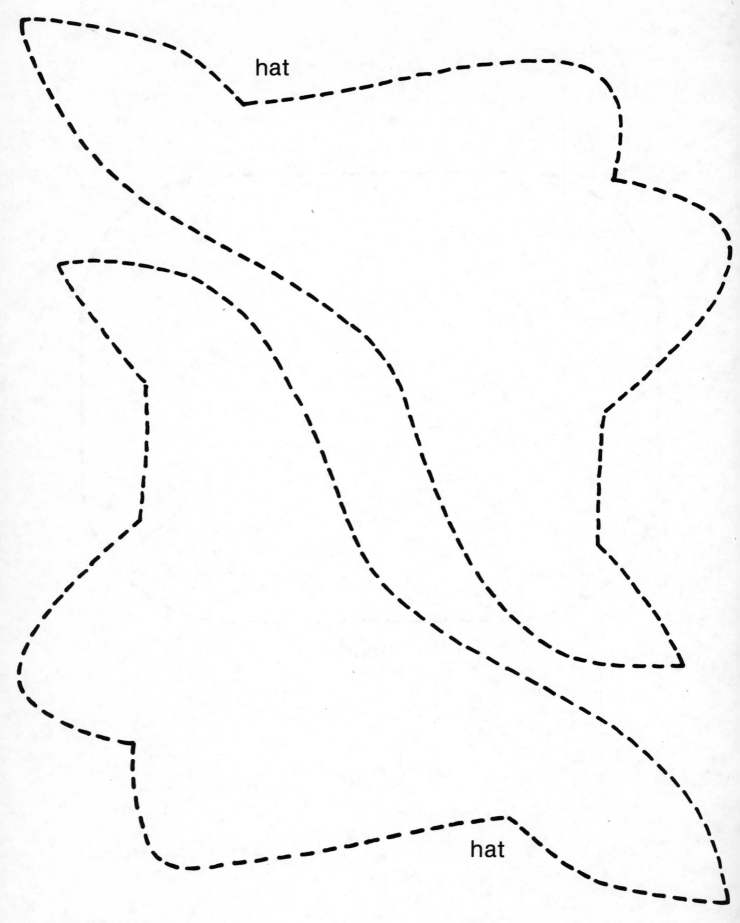

hat

hat

Pattern E (light brown)

Bagging It with Puppets! © 1988 David S. Lake Publishers

18 Scarecrow

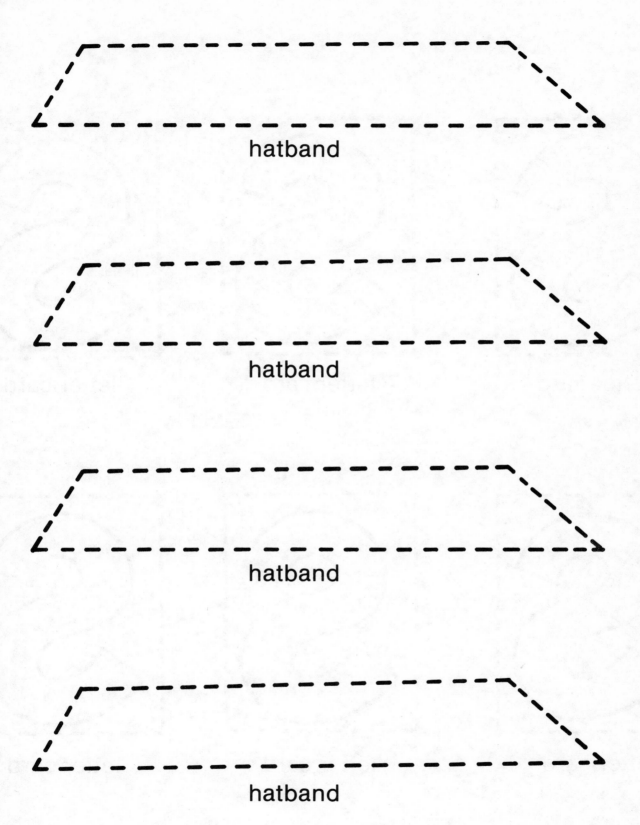

hatband

hatband

hatband

hatband

Pattern F (dark brown)

Scarecrow 19

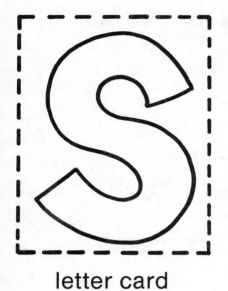

letter card

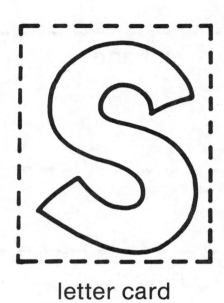

letter card

letter card

letter card

letter card

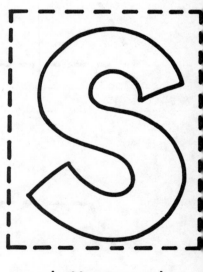

letter card

Pattern G (yellow)

Bagging It with Puppets! © 1988 David S. Lake Publishers

Tanya Tiger

Materials:

- paper lunch bags (11″ × 5¾″) for puppet base
- orange construction paper (head, body, arms)
- white construction paper (eyes, teeth)
- pink construction paper (tongue)
- crayons
- scissors
- paste
- paper clips
- paper cutter
- patterns on pages 23–28

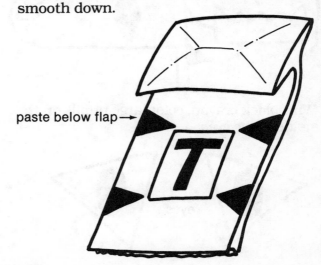

Preparation: ☆

1. Duplicate patterns on the appropriate colored construction paper.
2. For each child, make a packet containing:
   a) Pattern A (head)
   b) Pattern B (arms)
   c) Pattern C (body)
   d) one tongue from Pattern D
   e) one pair of eyes from Pattern E
   f) one row of teeth from Pattern F
   g) one paper lunch bag
   h) one paper clip
   Clip a–f together on the paper bag with the paper clip.

Procedure: ☆

1. Distribute to each student:
   a) paste
   b) crayons
   c) scissors
   d) puppet packet
   Demonstrate the following steps for the students.
2. Unclip the puppet packet and write your name on the back side of the paper lunch bag. Place the bag aside for now.
3. With black crayon, outline the interior lines of the puppet. Fill in all triangles and diamonds on the tiger with black. Fill in the paw circles with pink crayon, and outline them with black. Fill in the nose, the circles on the cheeks, and the letter *T* on the letter card with black crayon.
4. Cut all duplicated patterns along the dotted lines.
5. With one finger, put paste on the outside edge of the bag *(do not get paste on the flap)*. Place the body on the pasted edges and smooth down.

paste below flap →

6. Run paste along the edges of the tongue. Place the tongue over the body, curved side facing down. Do not get paste on the flap.

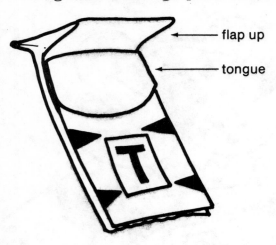

7. Run paste along the edges of the teeth. Attach the teeth to the bottom of the tongue, with the points facing up.

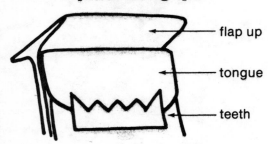

8. Apply paste to the inside edge of each arm. Attach the arms below the flap, in the crease of the bag.

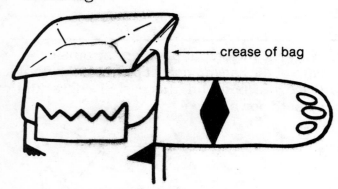

9. With black crayon, color large pupils on the inside of the eyes.

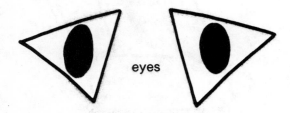

10. Run paste along the sides of the eyes. Place the eyes on each side of the nose.

11. Apply paste to the outside edge of the flap.

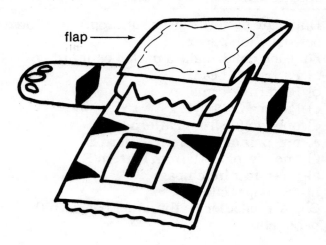

12. Place the head on the pasted flap. Smooth down.
13. Let the puppet dry before using.

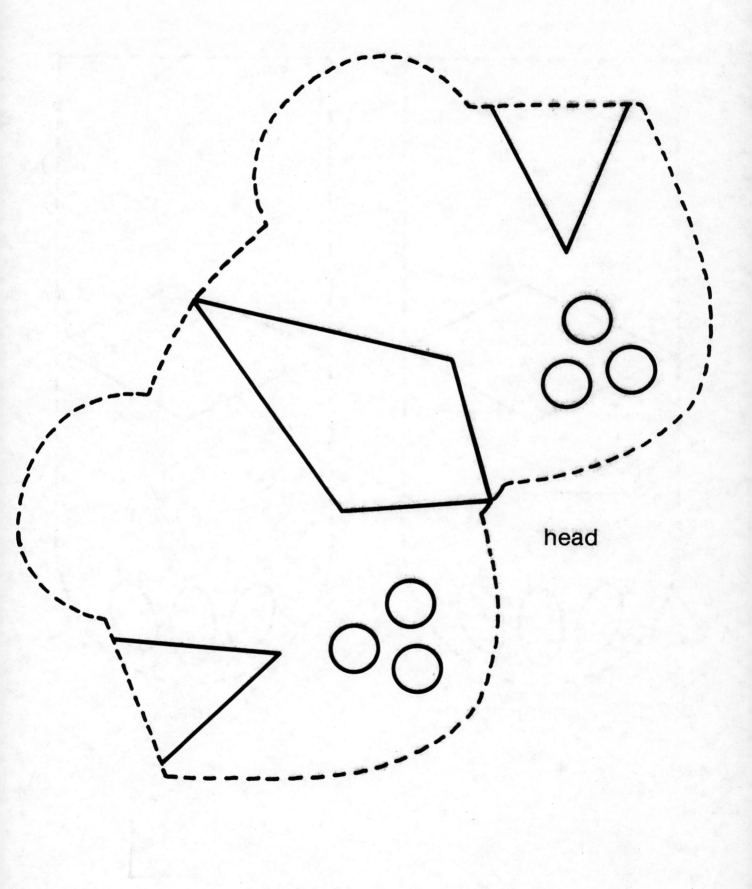

head

Pattern A (orange)

Tiger   23

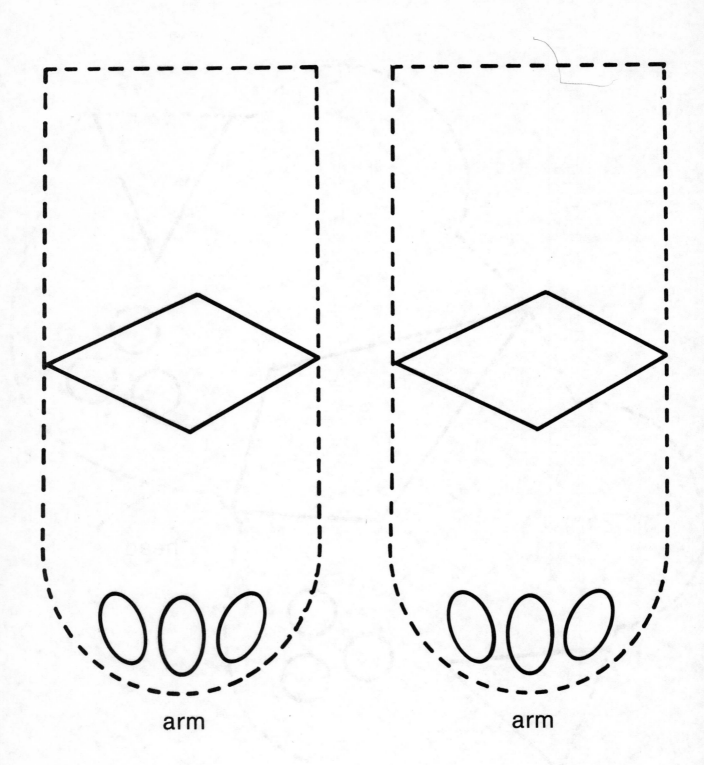

arm

arm

Bagging It with Puppets! © 1988 David S. Lake Publishers

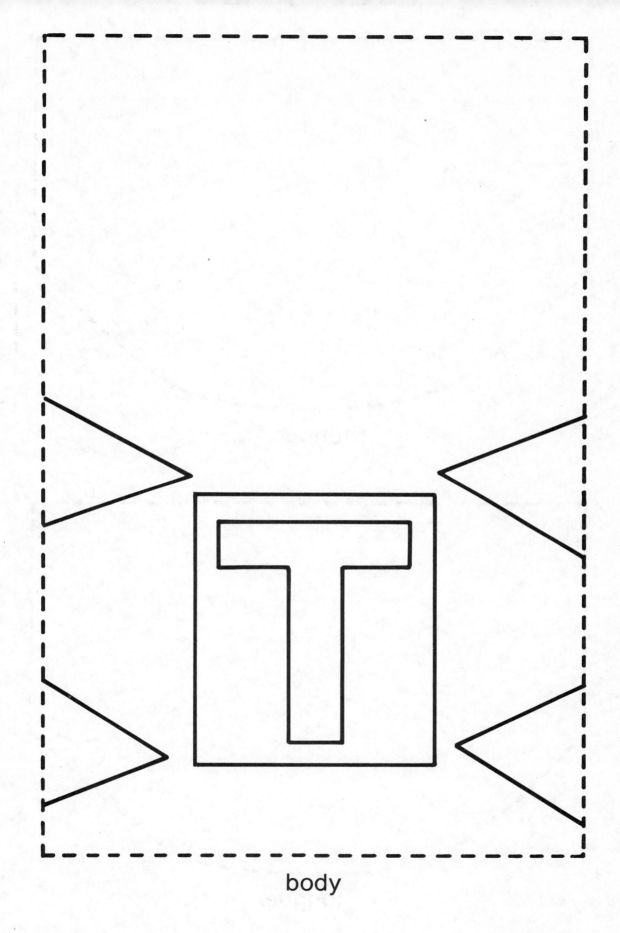

body

Pattern C (orange)

Tiger 25

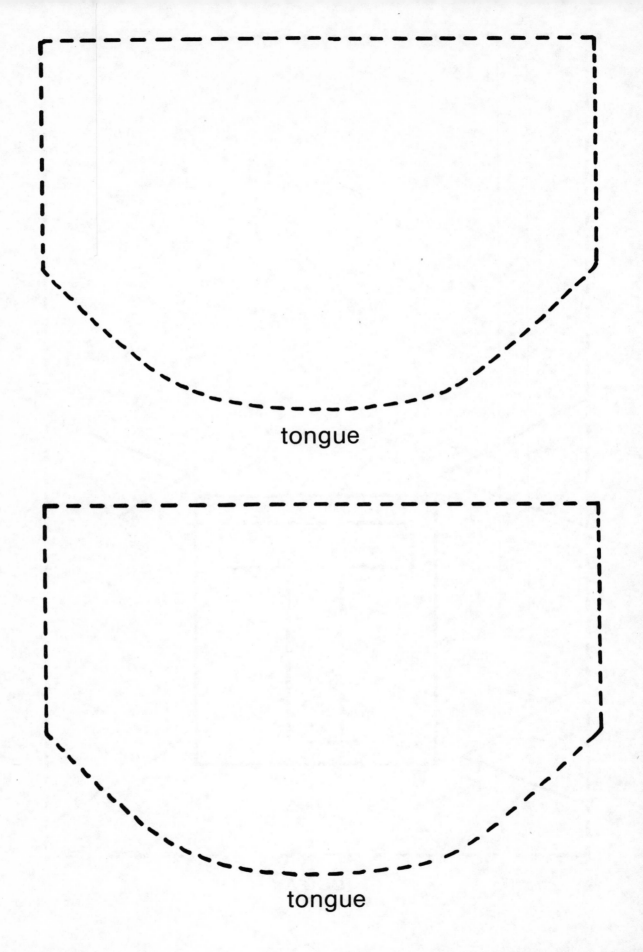

tongue

tongue

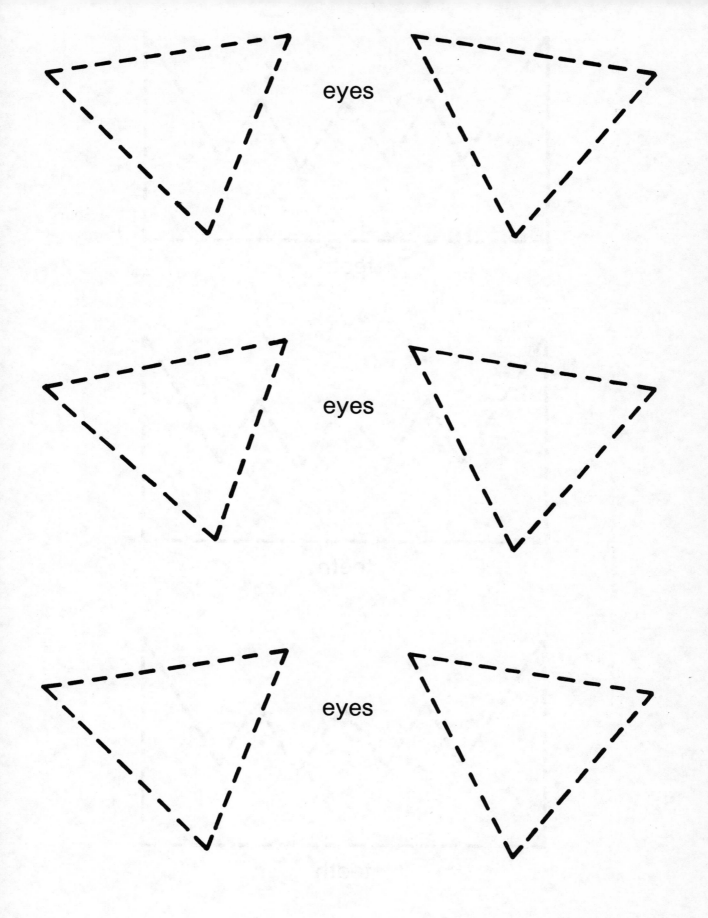

eyes

eyes

eyes

Pattern E (white)

Tiger 27

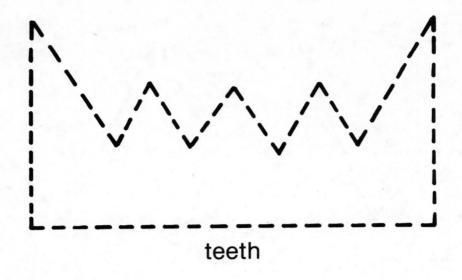

teeth

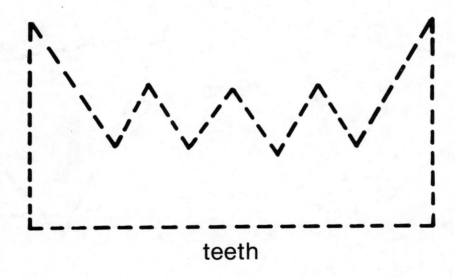

teeth

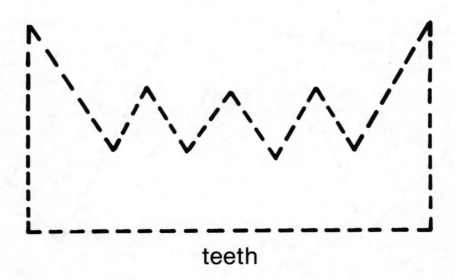

teeth

Merry Mouse

Materials: ☆

- paper lunch bags (11″ × 5¾″) for puppet base
- gray construction paper (body, outer ears, head, paws)
- pink construction paper (inner ears, letter card, nose)
- black construction paper (whiskers)
- crayons
- scissors
- paste
- paper clips
- paper cutter
- pink yarn
- patterns on pages 31–33

Preparation: ☆

1. Duplicate patterns on the appropriate colored construction paper.
2. Using a paper cutter, cut sheets of construction paper for:
   a) body (gray), 6″ × 9″
   b) whiskers (black), 2″ × 4″
   You can cut four to five sheets at a time.
3. For each child, make a packet containing:
   a) Pattern A (outer ears)
   b) Pattern B (head, paws)
   c) Pattern C (inner ears, letter card, nose)
   d) one precut body
   e) one precut rectangle for whiskers
   f) one 12″ piece of pink yarn for the tail
   g) one paper lunch bag
   h) one paper clip
   Clip a–f together on the paper bag with the paper clip.

Procedure: ☆

1. Distribute to each student:
   a) paste
   b) crayons
   c) scissors
   d) puppet packet
   Demonstrate the following steps for the students.
2. Unclip the puppet packet and write your name on the back side of the paper lunch bag. Place the bag aside for now.
3. With black crayon, color the letter *M* on the letter card.
4. Cut all duplicated patterns along the dotted lines.
5. With one finger, put paste on the outside edge of the bag (*do not get paste on the flap*). Place the body on the pasted edge and smooth down.

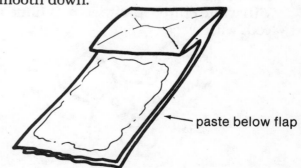

← paste below flap

6. Paste the letter card on the lower part of the body.

7. Run paste on the straight edge of the paws. Paste the upper paws below the flap, in the crease of the bag. Paste the lower paws at the bottom of the body, in the creases of the bag.

8. Run paste along the outside edge of each inner ear. Place the inner ears on the outer ears.

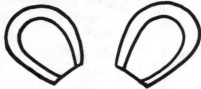

9. Run paste along the straight edge of each ear. Attach the ears to the back of the head.

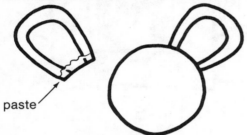

paste

10. Paste the nose on the head.

11. With white crayon, color two large ovals for eyes. Outline the eyes with black. Add pupils and lashes. With red crayon, draw a mouth. With white crayon, draw teeth. Outline the teeth with black crayon.

12. Cut the black 2″ × 4″ rectangle into whiskers, three for each side of the face. Paste the whiskers on the mouse's face.

13. Apply paste to the outside edge of the flap.

paste on flap

14. Place the head on the pasted flap and smooth down.

15. Paste the yarn tail to the center of the back side of the bag.

16. Let the puppet dry before using.

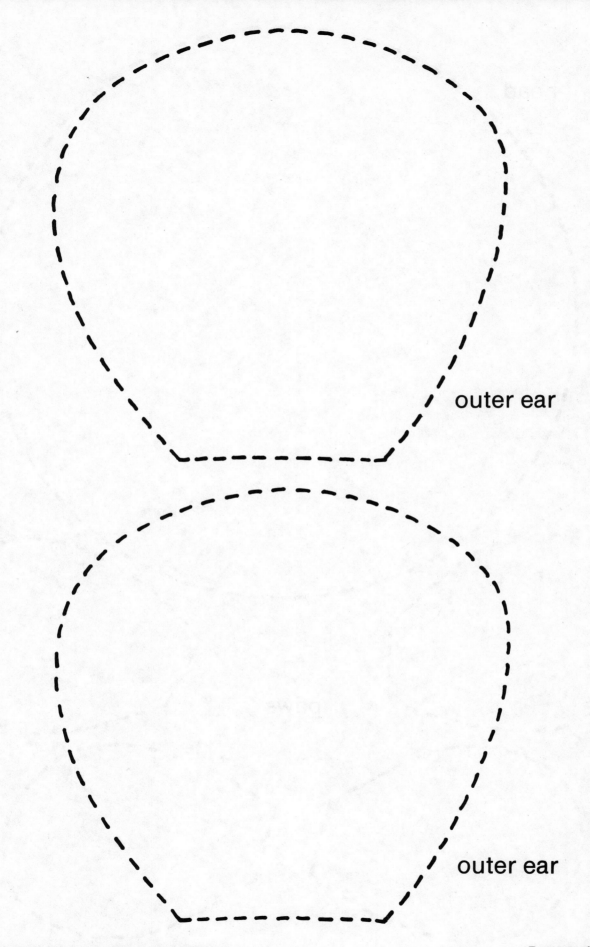

outer ear

outer ear

Pattern A (gray)

Mouse 31

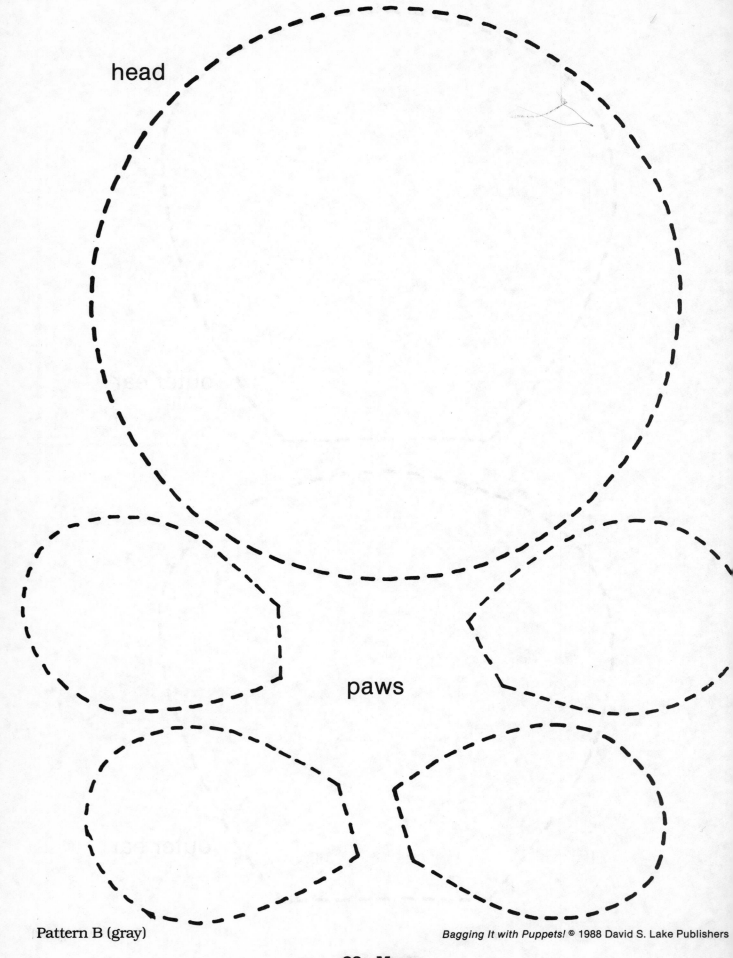

head

paws

Pattern B (gray)

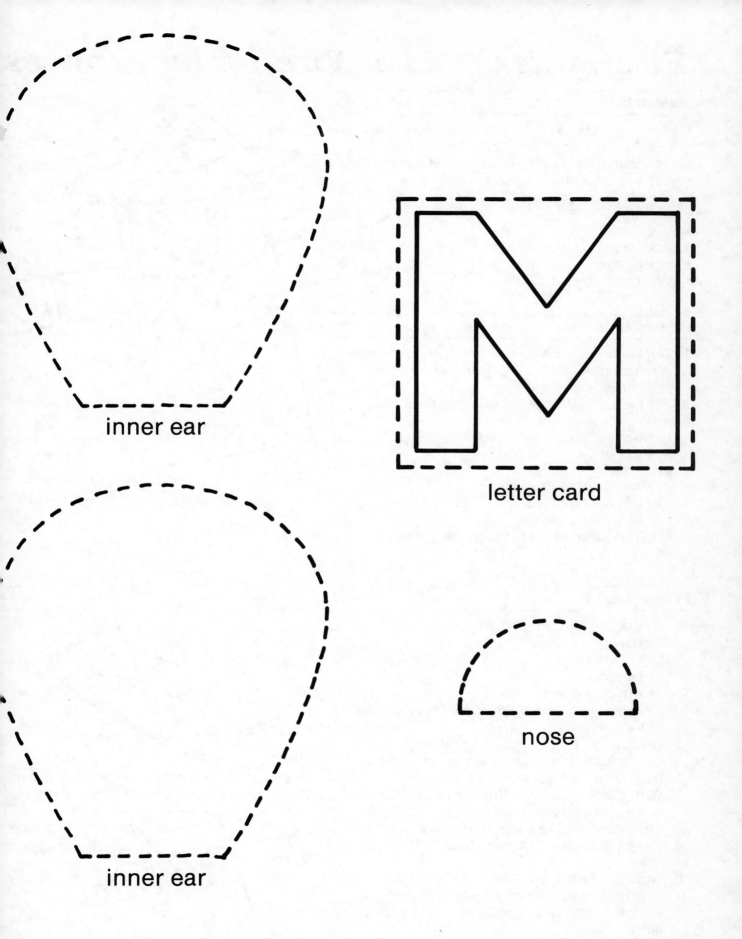

inner ear

letter card

inner ear

nose

Pattern C (pink)

Firefighter Fred or Firefighter Frances

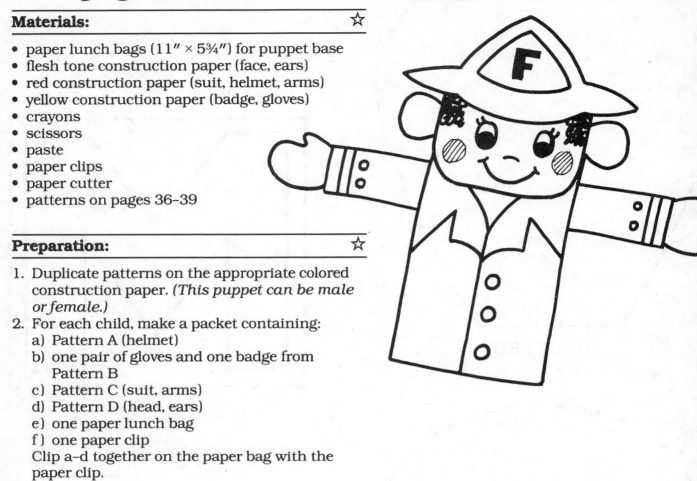

Materials: ☆

- paper lunch bags (11″ × 5¾″) for puppet base
- flesh tone construction paper (face, ears)
- red construction paper (suit, helmet, arms)
- yellow construction paper (badge, gloves)
- crayons
- scissors
- paste
- paper clips
- paper cutter
- patterns on pages 36–39

Preparation: ☆

1. Duplicate patterns on the appropriate colored construction paper. *(This puppet can be male or female.)*
2. For each child, make a packet containing:
   a) Pattern A (helmet)
   b) one pair of gloves and one badge from Pattern B
   c) Pattern C (suit, arms)
   d) Pattern D (head, ears)
   e) one paper lunch bag
   f) one paper clip
   Clip a–d together on the paper bag with the paper clip.

Procedure: ☆

1. Distribute to each student:
   a) paste
   b) crayons
   c) scissors
   d) puppet packet
   Demonstrate the following steps for the students.
2. Unclip the puppet packet and write your name on the back side of the paper lunch bag. Place the bag aside for now.
3. With black crayon, outline the interior lines of the suit and arms (buttons, too). Color in the letter *F* on the badge with black crayon.
4. Cut all duplicated patterns along the dotted lines.
5. With one finger, put paste on the outside edge of the bag *(do not get paste on the flap)*. Place the suit on the pasted edge and smooth down.

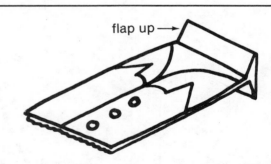

flap up →

6. Run paste along the inside edge of each arm. Attach the arms below the flap, in the creases of the bag.

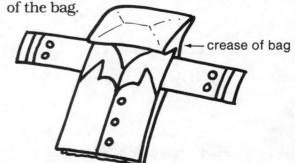

← crease of bag

7. Paste the gloves, thumbs up, behind the arms.

8. Paste the badge on the helmet.

9. Run paste along the straight edge of the head. Place the helmet on the pasted edge.

10. Run paste along the straight edge of each ear. Paste the ears below the helmet, on the back side of the head.

11. With crayons, add the facial features and the hair. With white crayon, color two large ovals for the eyes. Outline the eyes in black; add pupils and lashes. Add the nose. With red crayon, add the mouth. With black crayon, add the hair. Add cheeks with pink crayon.

12. Apply paste to the outside edge of the flap.

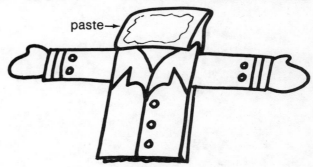

13. Place the head on the pasted flap.
14. Let the puppet dry before using.

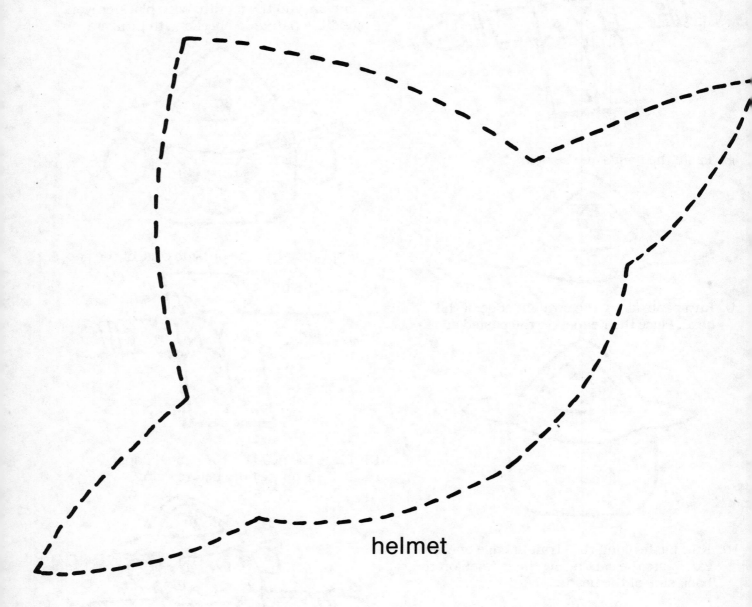

helmet

badge

gloves

gloves

badge

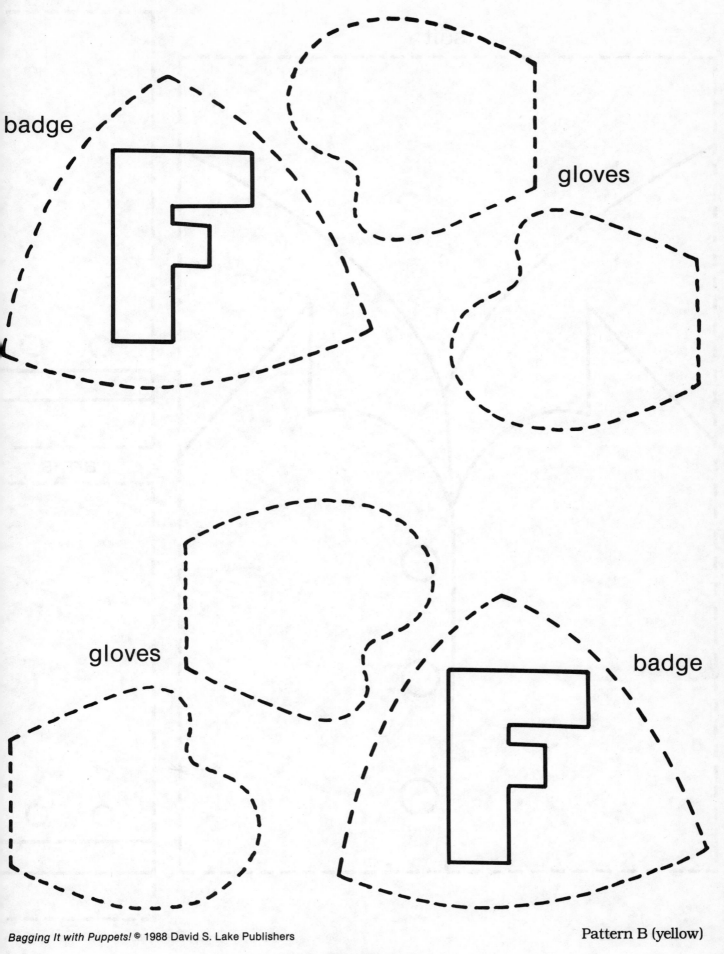

Pattern B (yellow)

Firefighter 37

suit

arms

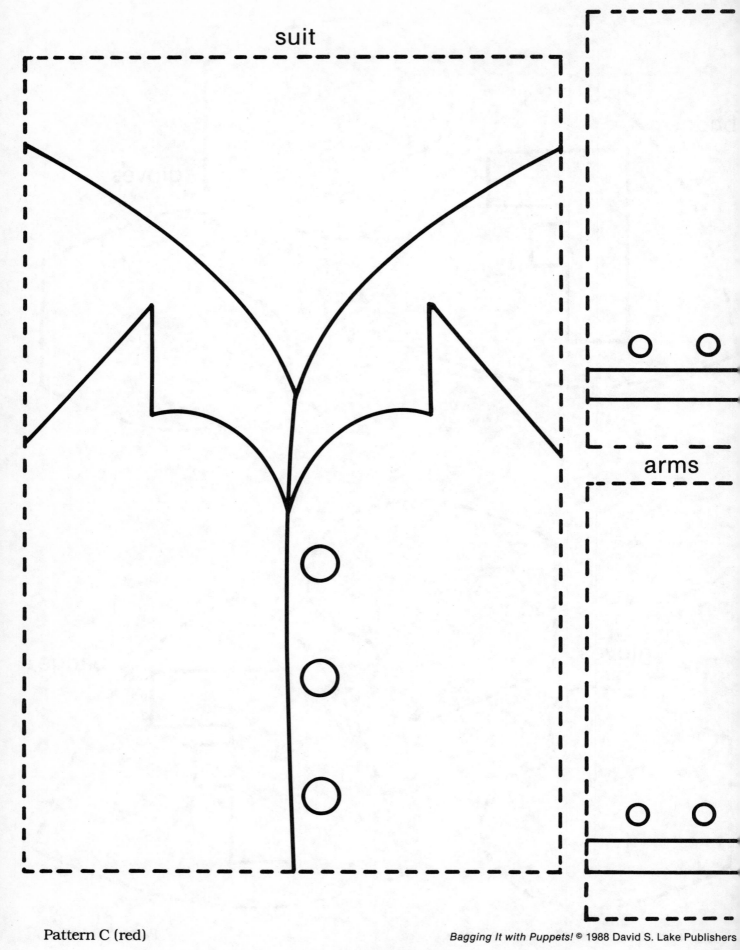

Pattern C (red)

38 Firefighter

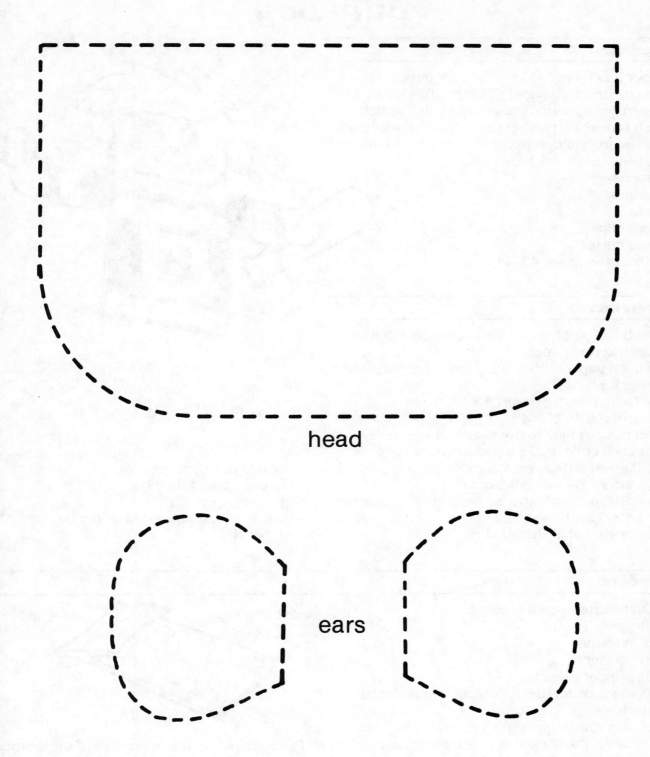

head

ears

Pattern D (flesh tone)

Billy Boy

Materials: ☆

- paper lunch bags (11″ × 5¾″) for puppet base
- red construction paper (T-shirt, arms)
- brown construction paper (baseball bat, hair)
- flesh tone construction paper (head, ears, hands)
- white construction paper (shirt stripes, cuff stripes, letter card, baseball)
- crayons
- scissors
- paste
- paper clips
- paper cutter
- patterns on pages 42–44

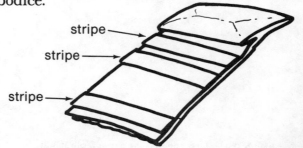

Preparation ☆

1. Duplicate patterns on the appropriate colored construction paper.
2. Using a paper cutter, cut sheets of construction paper for:
   a) T-shirt bodice (red), 6″ × 9″
   b) arms (red), 2″ × 4″
   You can cut four to five sheets at a time.
3. For each child, make a packet containing:
   a) Pattern A (face, ears, hands)
   b) Pattern B (baseball bat, hair)
   c) Pattern C (cuff stripes, shirt stripes, baseball, letter card)
   d) one precut T-shirt bodice
   e) two precut arms
   f) one paper lunch bag
   g) one paper clip
   Clip a–e together on the paper bag with the paper clip.

Procedure: ☆

1. Distribute to each student:
   a) paste
   b) crayons
   c) scissors
   d) puppet packet
   Demonstrate the following steps for the students.
2. Unclip the puppet packet and write your name on the back side of the paper lunch bag. Place the bag aside for now.
3. With black crayon, outline the interior lines of the baseball and color in the letter *B* on the letter card.
4. Cut all duplicated patterns along the dotted lines.
5. With one finger, put paste on the outside edge of the bag *(do not get paste on the flap).* Place the T-shirt bodice on the pasted edge and smooth down.

paste below flap

6. Paste stripes on the upper half of the T-shirt bodice.

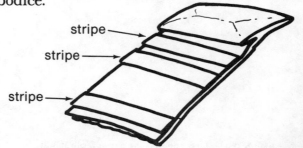

stripe
stripe
stripe

7. Paste the letter card below the upper stripes.
8. Run paste along the inside edge of each arm. Attach the arms below the flap, in the creases of the bag.

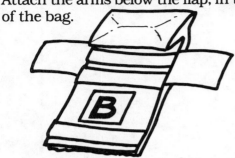

9. Paste a cuff stripe on the outside edge of each arm.

10. Apply paste to the inside edge of each hand. Attach the hands, thumbs up, behind the arms.

11. Run paste along the straight edge of the head. Place the hair on the head.

12. Apply paste to the straight edge of each ear. Paste the ears below the hair, on the back side of the head.

13. With crayons, add the facial features. With white crayon, color two large ovals for the eyes. Outline the eyes with black, and add pupils and lashes. With red crayon, draw the mouth. Add the nose with black crayon. Add cheeks with pink crayon.

14. Apply paste to the outside edge of the flap. Place the head on the pasted flap and smooth down.

paste

15. Paste the baseball under one hand.
16. Paste the bat under one hand.
17. Let the puppet dry before using.

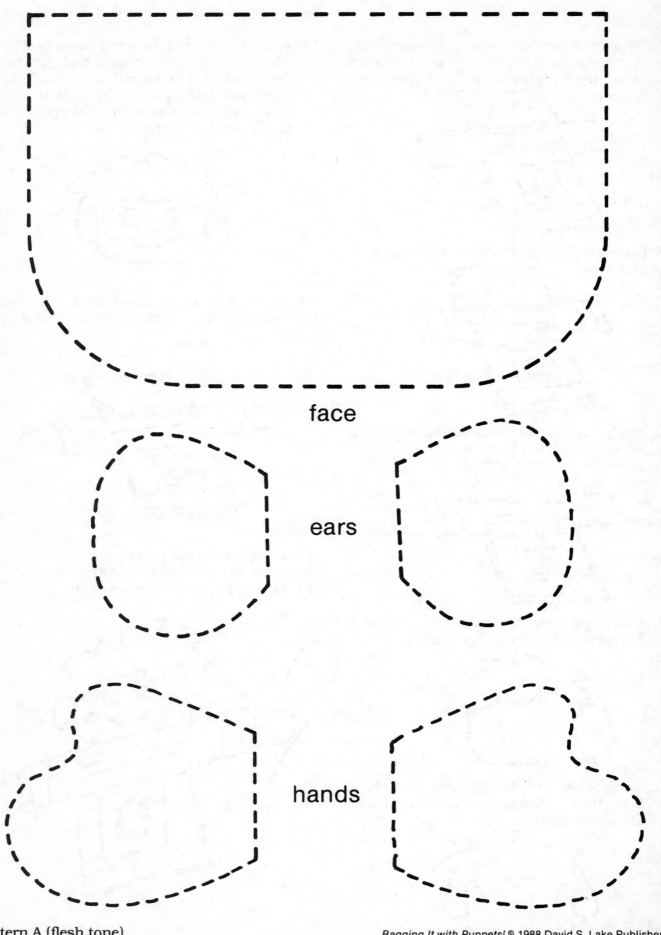

face

ears

hands

Pattern A (flesh tone)

Bagging It with Puppets! © 1988 David S. Lake Publishers

42 Boy

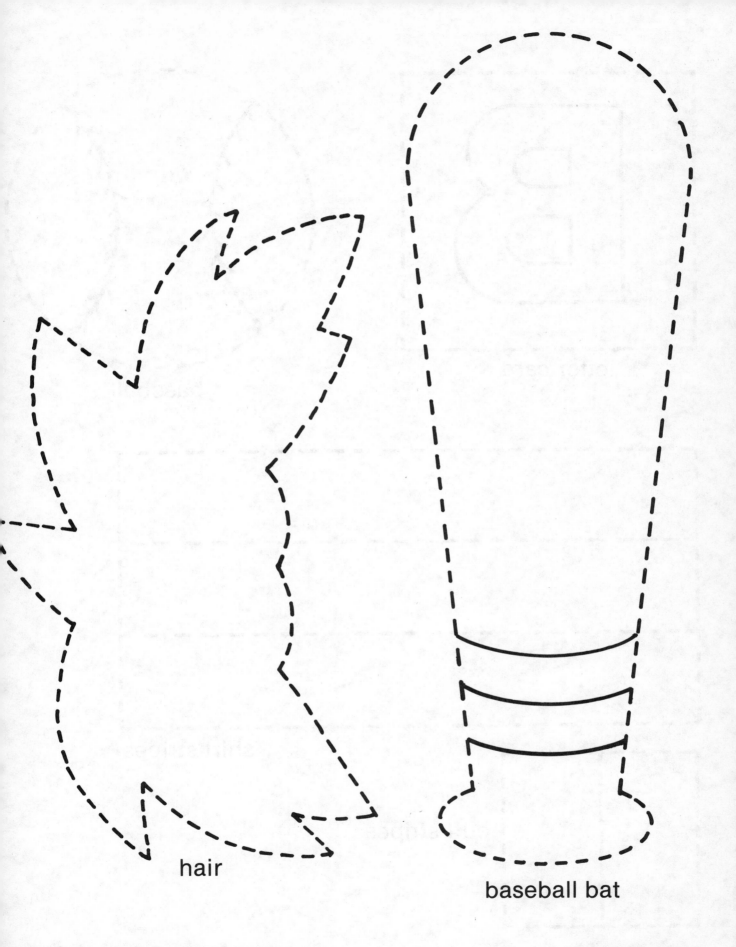

hair

baseball bat

Pattern B (brown)

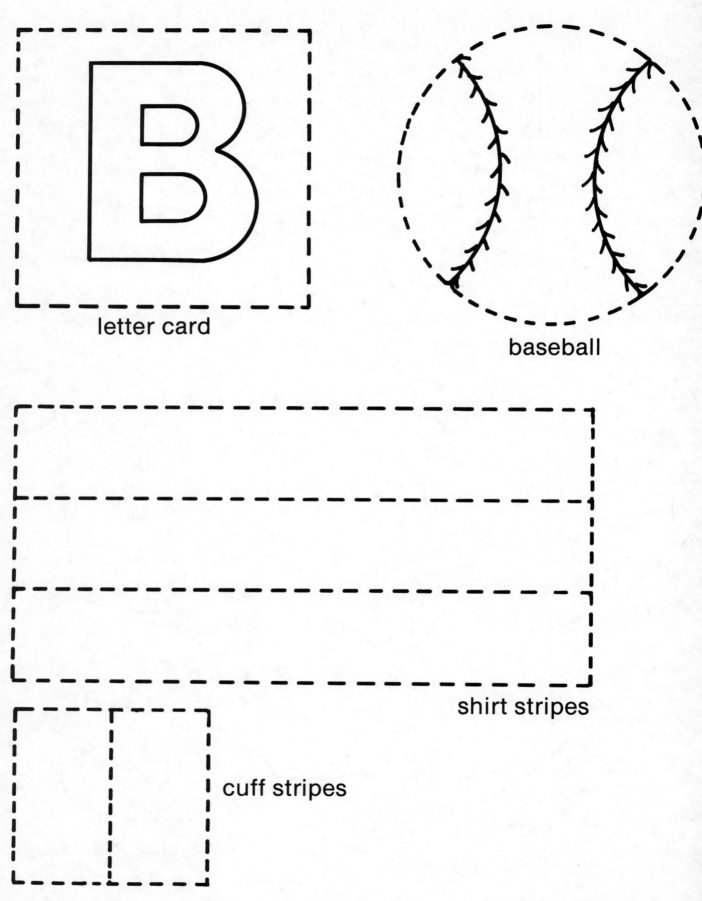

letter card

baseball

shirt stripes

cuff stripes

Pattern C (white)

Cowboy Curly or Cowgirl Chris

Materials: ☆

- paper lunch bags (11″ × 5¾″) for puppet base
- red construction paper (bandanna)
- flesh tone construction paper (head, ears, hands)
- light blue construction paper (shirt, sleeves)
- brown construction paper (hat)
- black construction paper (Cowgirl Chris's hair)
- crayons
- scissors
- paste
- paper clips
- paper cutter
- patterns on pages 48–52

Preparation: ☆

1. Duplicate patterns on the appropriate colored construction paper.
2. For each child, make a packet containing:
   a) Pattern A (head, hands, ears)
   b) Pattern B (bandanna)
   c) Pattern C (shirt, sleeves)
   d) Pattern D (hat)
   e) Pattern E *(hair for Cowgirl Chris only)*
   f) one paper lunch bag
   g) one paper clip
   Clip a–e together on the paper bag with the paper clip.

Procedure: ☆

1. Distribute to each student:
   a) paste
   b) crayons
   c) scissors
   d) puppet packet
   Demonstrate the following steps for the students.
2. Unclip the puppet packet and write your name on the back side of the paper lunch bag. Place the bag aside for now.
3. With black crayon, outline the interior lines of the shirt and the sleeves. Color in the buttons. Outline the bandanna with black crayon, and add a design of circles to it with black and white crayons. Color in the letter *C* on the pocket with black crayon.
4. Cut all duplicated patterns along the dotted lines.

5. With one finger, put paste on the outside edge of the bag *(do not get paste on the flap)*. Place the shirt on the pasted edge and smooth down.

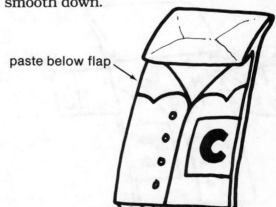

paste below flap

6. Run paste along the inside edge of each sleeve. Attach the sleeves below the flap, in the creases of the bag.

7. Run paste along the top edge of the shirt, under the flap.

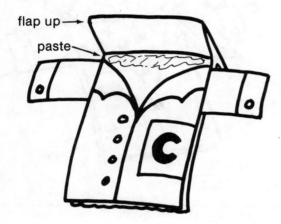

8. Place the bandanna on the shirt and smooth down.

9. Put paste on the inside edge of each hand. Attach the hands, thumbs up, behind the sleeves.

10. With red crayon, color in the hatband.

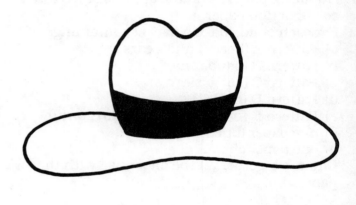

11. If you are making Cowgirl Chris, run paste along the straight edge of the head. Place the hair on the pasted edge.

12. Run paste along the top of the head. Place the hat on the pasted edge.

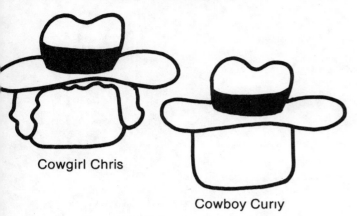

Cowgirl Chris

Cowboy Curly

13. If you are making Cowboy Curly, run paste along the straight edge of each ear. Paste the ears below the hat, on the back side of the head. (Cowgirl Chris does not require ears.)

14. With crayons, add the facial features. With white crayon, draw large ovals for the eyes. Outline the eyes with black and add pupils and lashes. Add the nose. With red crayon, add the mouth. Add cheeks with pink crayon. For Cowboy Curly, draw curly hair under the brim of the hat. You may add whiskers to Cowboy Curly with black crayon.

Cowgirl Chris

Cowboy Curly

15. Apply paste to the outside edge of the flap.

paste →

16. Place the head on the pasted flap.
17. Let the puppet dry before using.

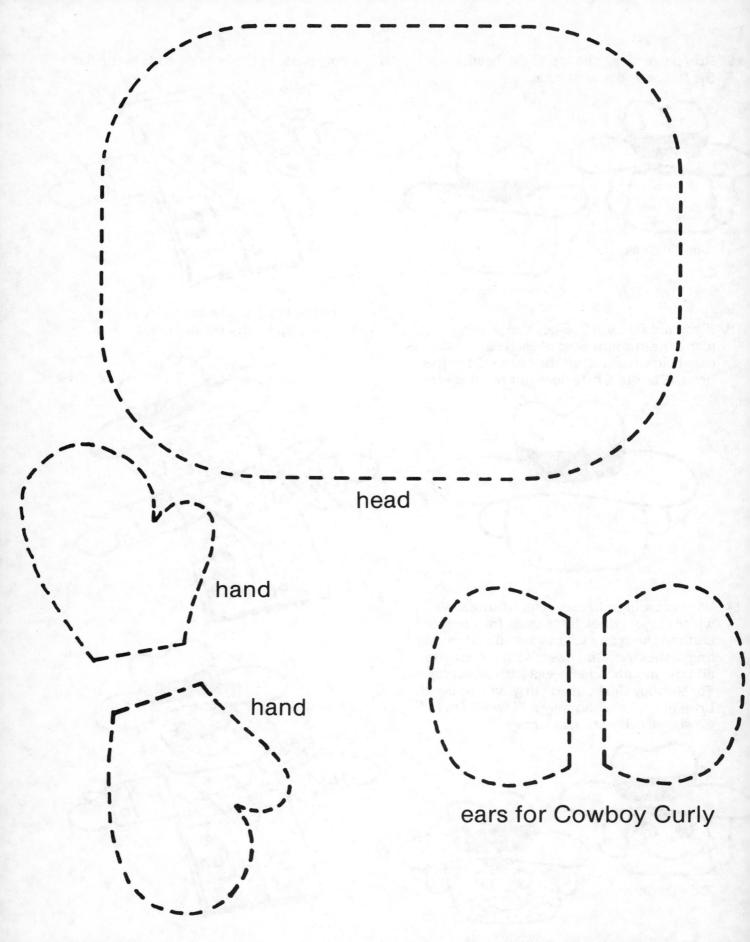

head

hand

hand

ears for Cowboy Curly

Pattern A (flesh tone)

Bagging It with Puppets! © 1988 David S. Lake Publishers

48 Cowboy/Cowgirl

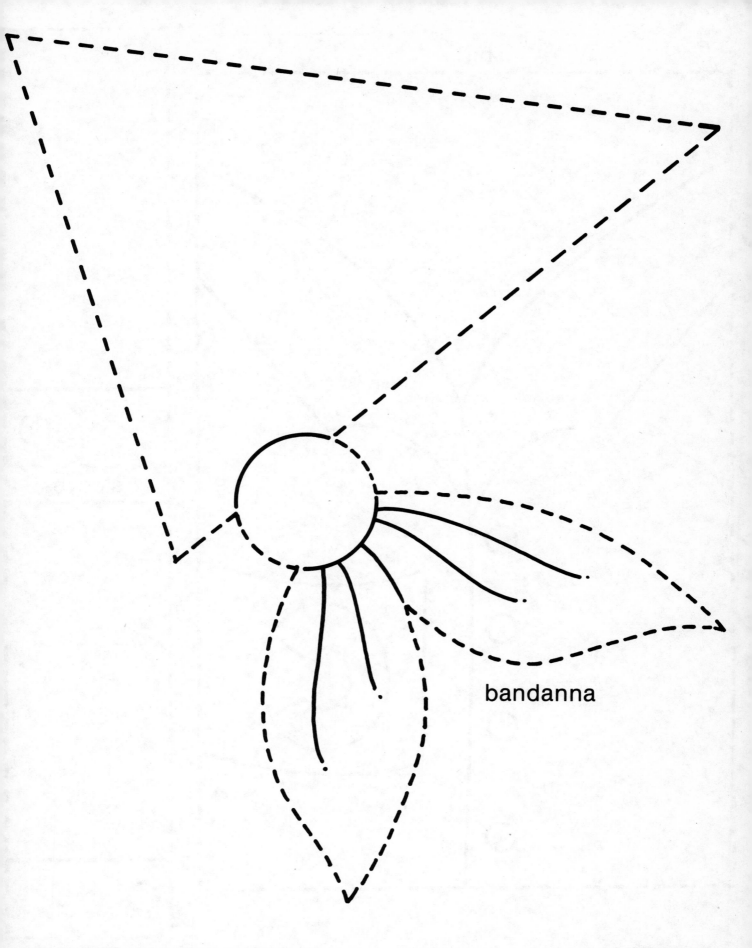

bandanna

Pattern B (red)

shirt

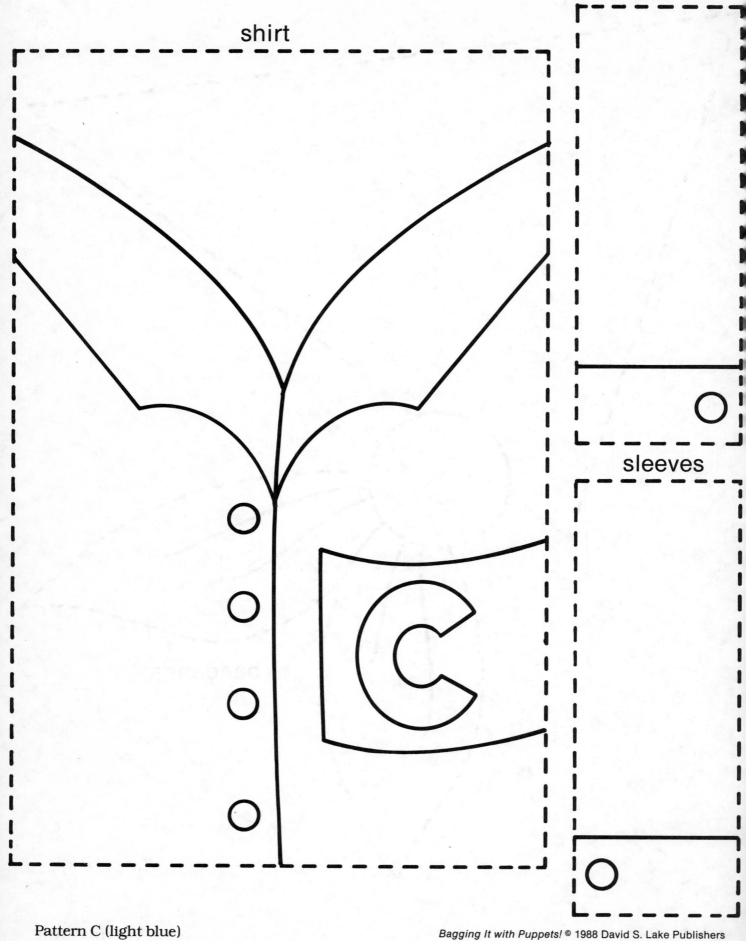

sleeves

Pattern C (light blue)

50   Cowboy/Cowgirl

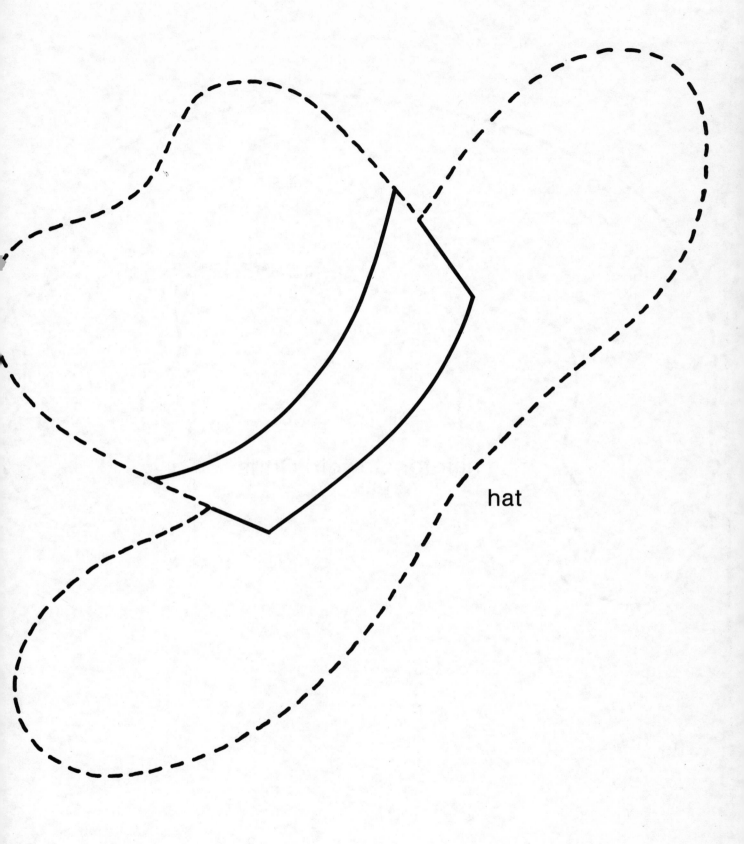

hat

Pattern D (brown)

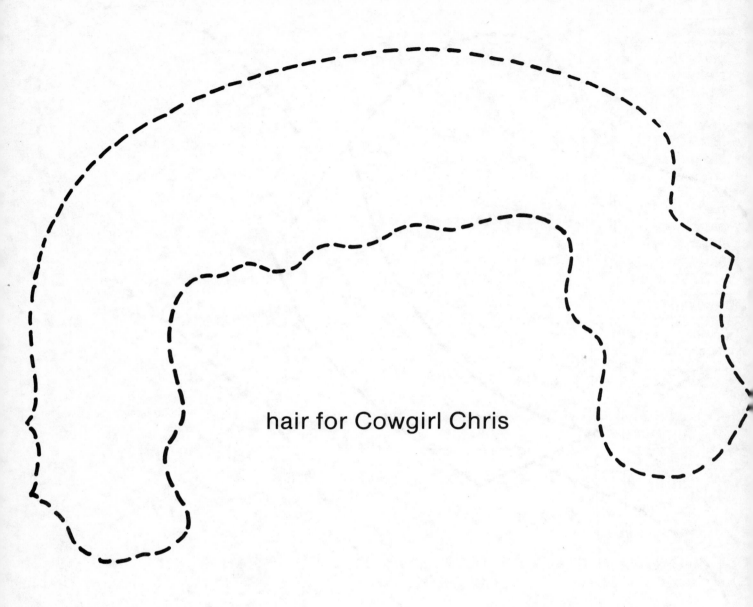

hair for Cowgirl Chris

Pattern E (black)

Doctor Donna or Doctor Dan

Materials:

- paper lunch bags (11″ × 5¾″) for puppet base
- white construction paper (jacket, arms, stethoscope)
- dark brown construction paper (hair)
- flesh tone construction paper (head, ears, hands)
- black (headpiece bands)
- aluminum foil (headpiece)
- crayons
- scissors
- paste
- paper clips
- paper cutter
- patterns on pages 56–60

Preparation:

1. Duplicate patterns on the appropriate colored construction paper.
2. Using a paper cutter, cut sheets of black construction paper 3″ × ½″ for the headpiece bands. You can cut four to five sheets at a time.
3. Cut out the headpiece pattern (Pattern E) and use it to trace circles on aluminum foil. Cut out the aluminum foil circles, one for each student. *(Don't forget to cut out the inner circle as well.)*
4. For each child, make a packet containing:
   a) Pattern A (jacket)
   b) Pattern B (head, ears, hands)
   c) Pattern C (hair—Doctor Donna or Doctor Dan)
   d) Pattern D (stethoscope, arms)
   e) one headpiece circle of aluminum foil
   f) two 3″ × ½″ sheets of black paper for the headpiece band
   g) one paper lunch bag
   h) one paper clip
   Clip a–f together on the paper bag with the paper clip.

Procedure:

1. Distribute to each student:
   a) paste
   b) crayons
   c) scissors
   d) puppet packet
   Demonstrate the following steps for the students.
2. Unclip the puppet packet and write your name on the back side of the paper lunch bag. Place the bag aside for now.

3. With black crayon, outline the interior lines of the jacket, the buttons, and the letter *D*. Color in the buttons and the letter *D* with black crayon. Color in the black part of the stethoscope.
4. Cut all duplicated patterns along the dotted lines.

5. With one finger, put paste on the outside edge of the bag (*do not get paste on the flap*). Place the jacket on the pasted edge and smooth down.

paste below flap →

6. Apply paste to the inside edge of each arm. Attach the arms below the flap, in the creases of the bag.

7. Paste the hands, thumbs up, behind the arms.

8. Run paste along the straight edge of the head. Attach the hair (*select either Doctor Donna's hair or Doctor Dan's hair*).

Doctor Donna

Doctor Dan

9. Run paste along the straight edge of each ear if you are making Doctor Dan. Paste the ears below the hair on the back side of the head. (*Doctor Donna does not need ears.*)

10. Run paste along the two strips of 3″ × ½″ black construction paper. Paste the two strips on the hair to form the headpiece band. Trim the edges.

11. Apply paste to the foil circle (headpiece) and paste it over the black strips.

12. With crayons, add the facial features. With white crayon, draw two large ovals for the eyes. Outline the eyes with black and add lashes and pupils. Add the nose. With red crayon, add the mouth.

13. Apply paste to the outside edge of the flap. Place the head on the pasted edge. Smooth down.

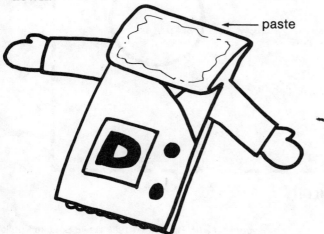

paste

14. Paste the stethoscope on the puppet's hand.
15. Let the puppet dry before using.

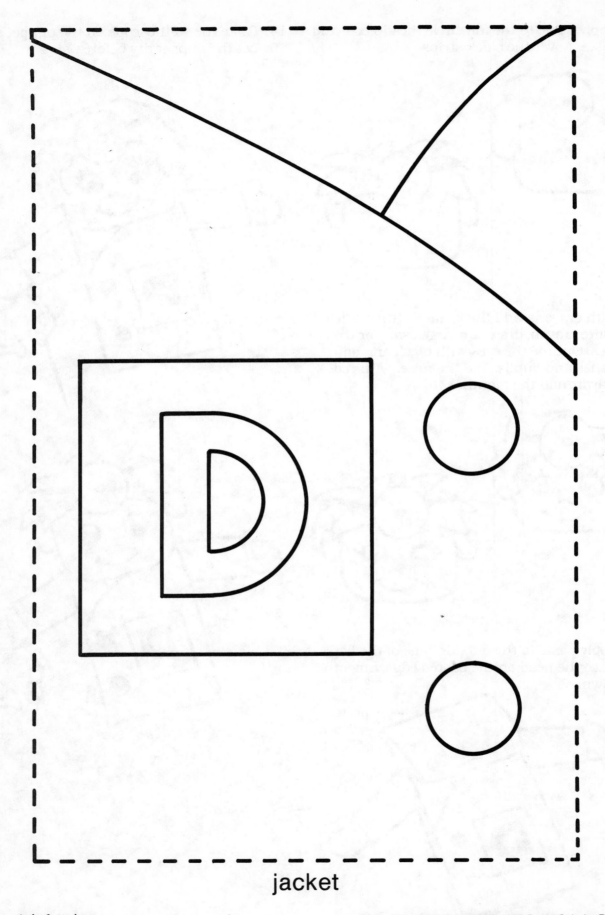

jacket

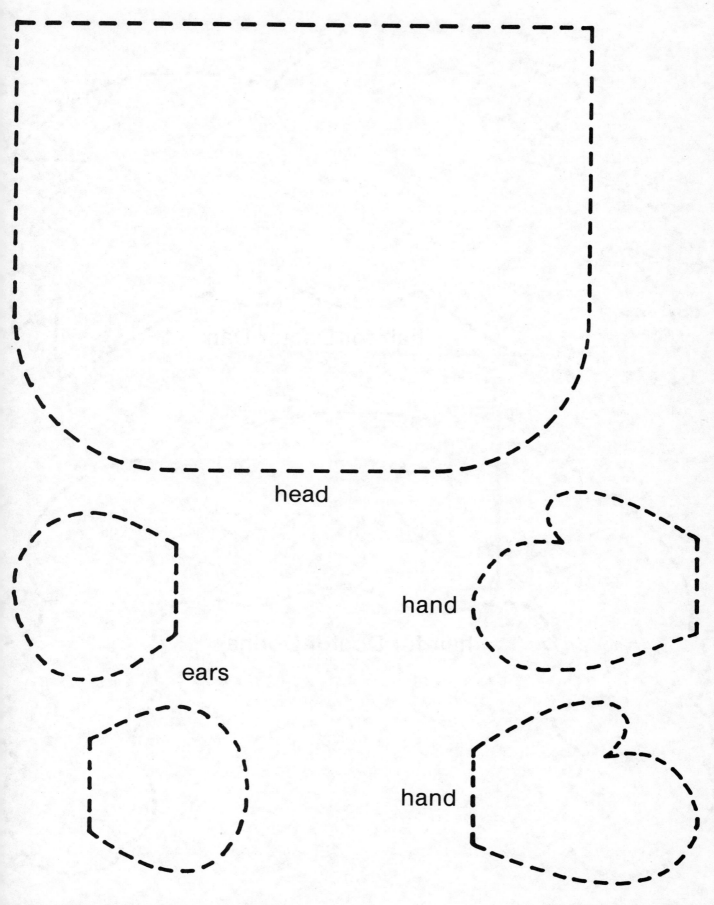

head

ears

hand

hand

Pattern B (flesh tone)

Doctor 57

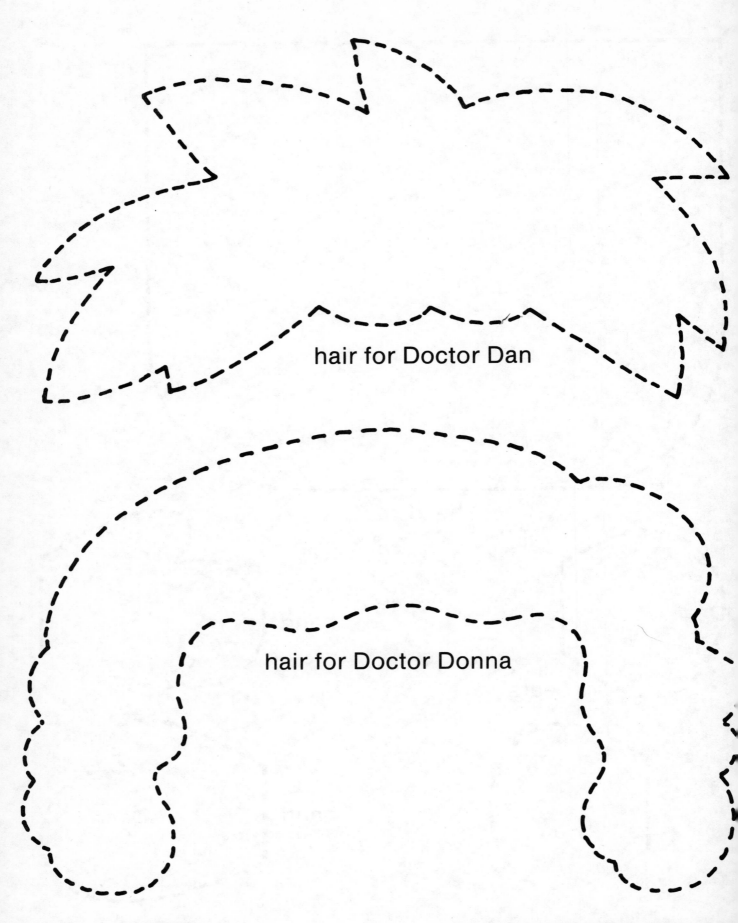

hair for Doctor Dan

hair for Doctor Donna

Pattern C (dark brown)

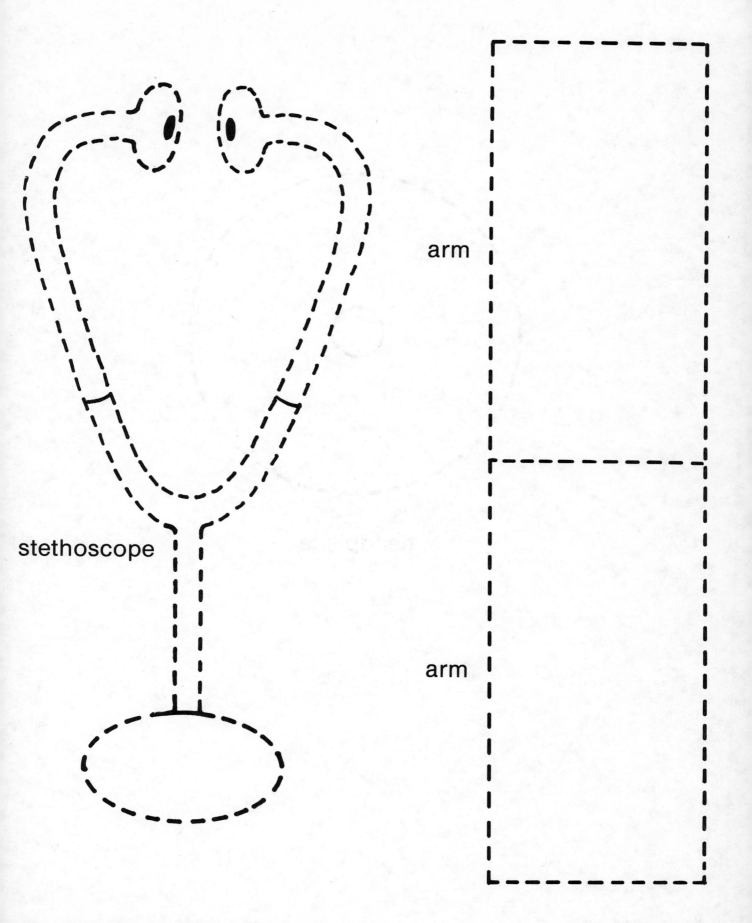

stethoscope

arm

arm

Pattern D (white)

Doctor 59

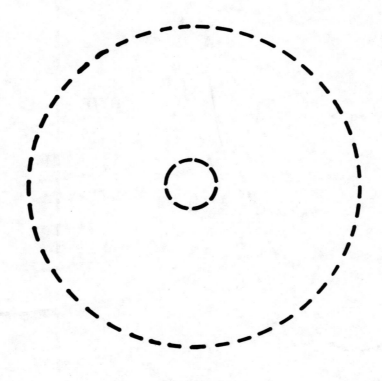

headpiece

Greta Girl

Materials: ☆

- paper lunch bags (11″ × 5 ¾″) for puppet base
- green construction paper (dress, arms)
- flesh tone construction paper (head, chest, hands)
- black construction paper (hair)
- white construction paper (letter card)
- green yarn for bows
- crayons
- scissors
- paste
- paper clips
- paper cutter
- patterns on pages 63–68

Preparation: ☆

1. Duplicate patterns on the appropriate colored construction paper.
2. Make one yarn bow for each puppet.
3. For each child, make a packet containing:
   a) Pattern A (dress)
   b) Pattern B (arms)
   c) Pattern C (hair)
   d) Pattern D (chest, hands)
   e) Pattern E (head)
   f) one letter card from Pattern F
   g) one yarn bow
   h) one paper lunch bag
   i) one paper clip
   Clip a–g together on the paper bag with the paper clip.

Procedure: ☆

1. Distribute to each student:
   a) paste
   b) crayons
   c) scissors
   d) puppet packet
   Demonstrate the following steps for the students.
2. Unclip the puppet packet and write your name on the back side of the paper lunch bag. Place the bag aside for now.
3. With black crayon, fill in the border around the puppet's dress and sleeves. Color in the letter *G* on the letter card with black crayon.

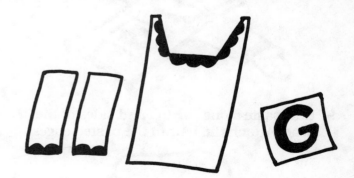

4. Cut all duplicated patterns along the dotted lines.

5. With one finger, put paste on the outside edge of the bag *(do not get paste on the flap)*. Place the chest on the pasted edge below the flap.

— chest

6. With one finger, put paste on the outside edge of the bag *(do not get paste on the flap)*. Place the dress on the pasted edges and smooth down. Paste the letter card on the dress.

7. Apply paste to the inside edge of each arm. Attach the arms below the flap, in the creases of the bag.

— paste

8. Paste the hands, thumbs up, behind the arms.

9. Run paste along the top and sides of the head. Attach the hair to the pasted edges.

10. With crayons, add the facial features. With white crayons, draw two large ovals for eyes. Outline the eyes with black crayons and add pupils and lashes. Add the nose. With red crayon, draw the mouth. Add cheeks with pink crayon.

11. Paste the green yarn bow to the hair.

12. Apply paste to the outside edge of the bag's flap.

paste on flap →

13. Place the head on the pasted flap.
14. Let the puppet dry before using.

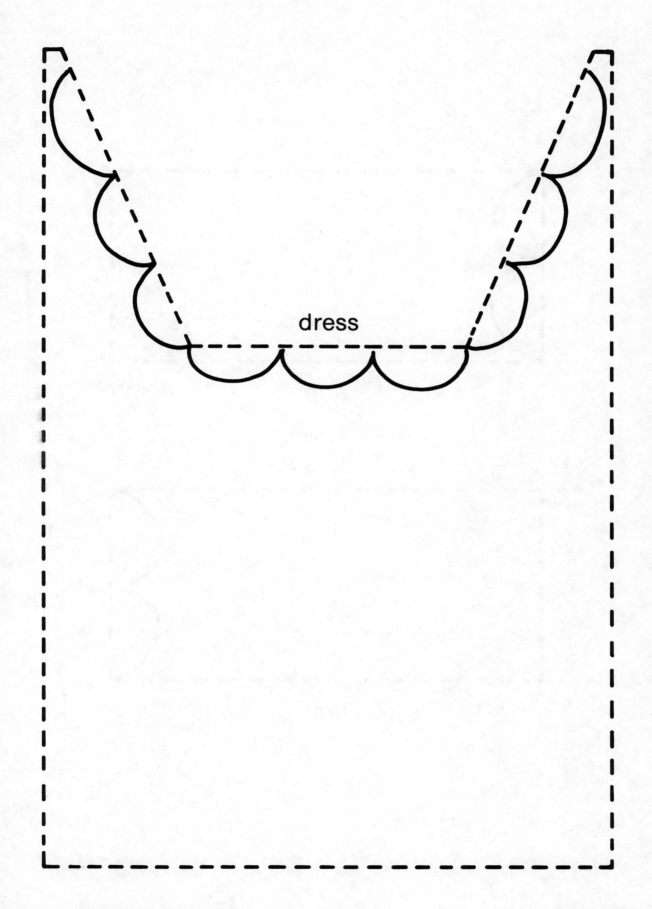

dress

Pattern A (green)

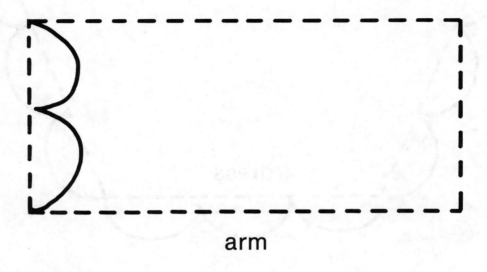

arm

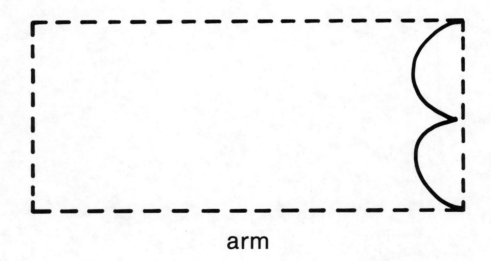

arm

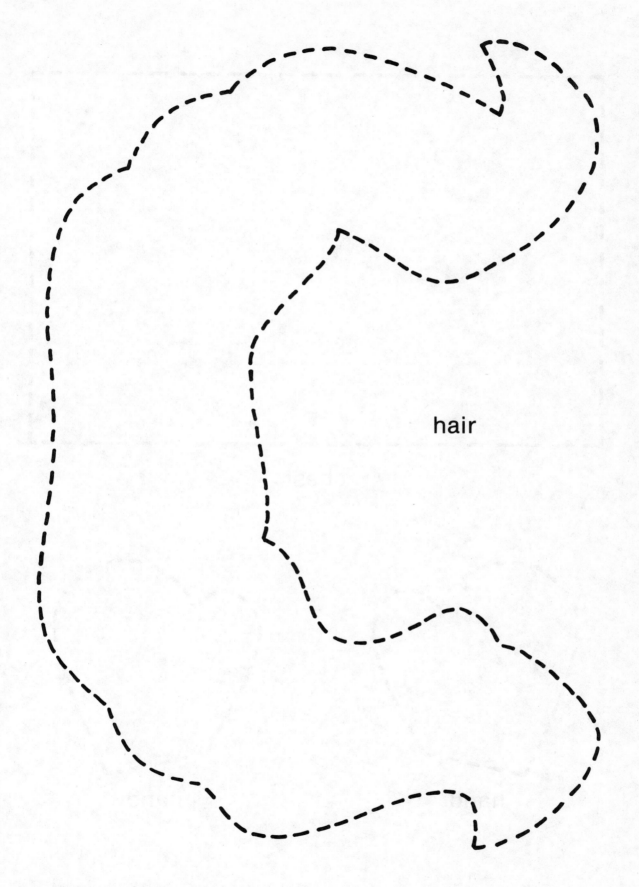

hair

Pattern C (black)

Girl 65

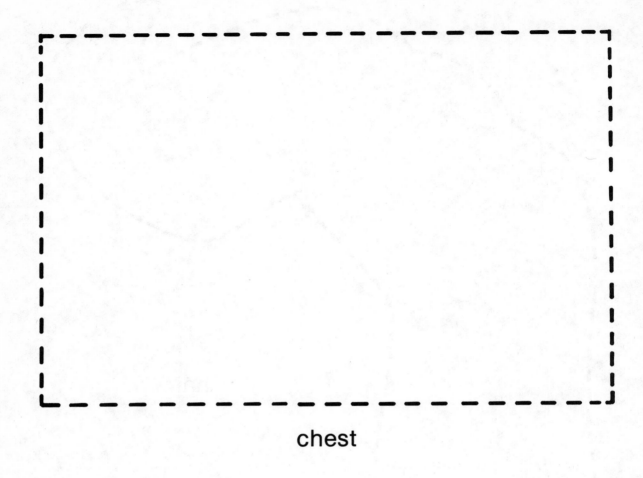

chest

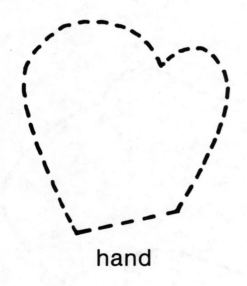

hand

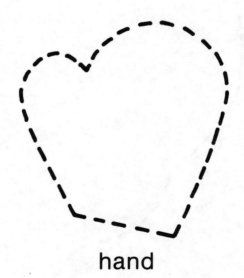

hand

Pattern D (flesh tone)

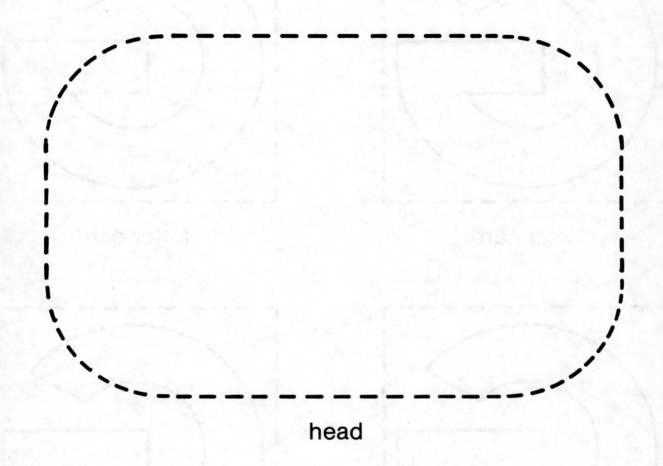

head

Pattern E (flesh tone)

letter card

letter card

letter card

letter card

Pattern F (white)

Harry Hippopotamus

Materials: ☆

- paper lunch bags (11″ × 5¾″) for puppet base
- gray construction paper (head, jaw, ears)
- red construction paper (tongue)
- white construction paper (eyes, teeth, letter card)
- black construction paper (pupils)
- crayons
- scissors
- paste
- paper clips
- paper cutter
- patterns on pages 71–75

Preparation: ☆

1. Duplicate patterns on the appropriate colored construction paper.
2. Using a paper cutter, cut sheets of construction paper for:
   a) two teeth (white), 1″ × 1½″
   b) two eyes (white), 2″ × 2½″
   c) two pupils (black), 1½″ × 2″
   You can cut four to five sheets at a time.
3. For each child, make a packet containing:
   a) Pattern A (jaw)
   b) Pattern B (head)
   c) Pattern C (tongue)
   d) one pair of ears from Pattern D
   e) one letter card from Pattern E
   f) two precut teeth
   g) two precut pieces for eyes
   h) two precut pieces for pupils
   i) one paper lunch bag
   j) one paper clip
   Clip a–h together on the paper bag with the paper clip.

Procedure: ☆

1. Distribute to each student:
   a) paste   c) scissors
   b) crayons   d) puppet packet
   Demonstrate the following steps for the students.
2. Unclip the puppet packet and write your name on the back side of the paper lunch bag. Place the bag aside for now.
3. With black crayon, outline the interior lines of the face (nose and dots). Color the letter *H* on the letter card black.
4. Cut all duplicated patterns along the dotted lines.
5. Place the two black rectangles (pupils) together. With scissors, shape the pupils by rounding all the corners.

6. With one finger, put paste on the outside edge of the bag (*do not get paste on the flap*). Place the jaw on the pasted edge and smooth down.

jaw →

7. With one finger, put paste on one side of the tongue. Place the tongue on top of the jaw, lining up the straight edge of the jaw and the straight edge of the tongue.

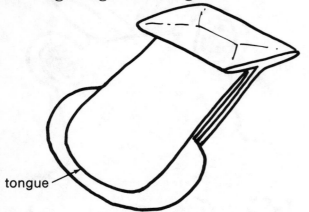

tongue

8. Paste the two teeth (white rectangles) on the bottom of the tongue, about four inches apart.

9. With scissors, shape the white rectangles into eyes by placing them together and rounding the edges. Paste the white eyes in the center of the two bulges on the face. Paste the black pupils in the center of the white eyes.

10. Put paste on the bottom part of the ears only. Place the ears behind the top of the head.

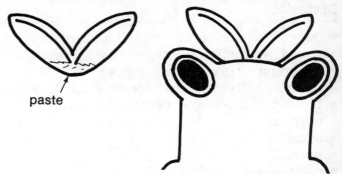

paste

11. Paste the letter card on the inside of the puppet's mouth, above the teeth.

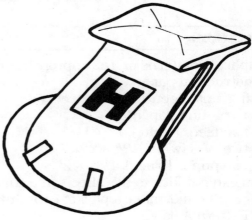

12. Apply paste to the outside edge of the flap.

paste →

13. Place the head on the flap.
14. Let the puppet dry before using.

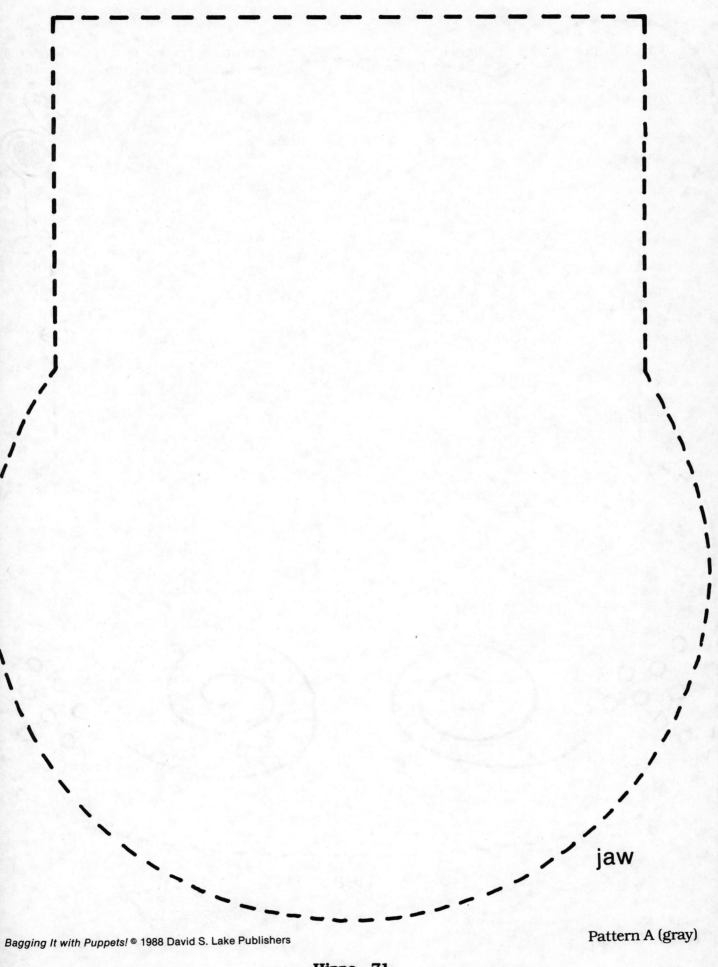

jaw

Pattern A (gray)

Hippo   71

head

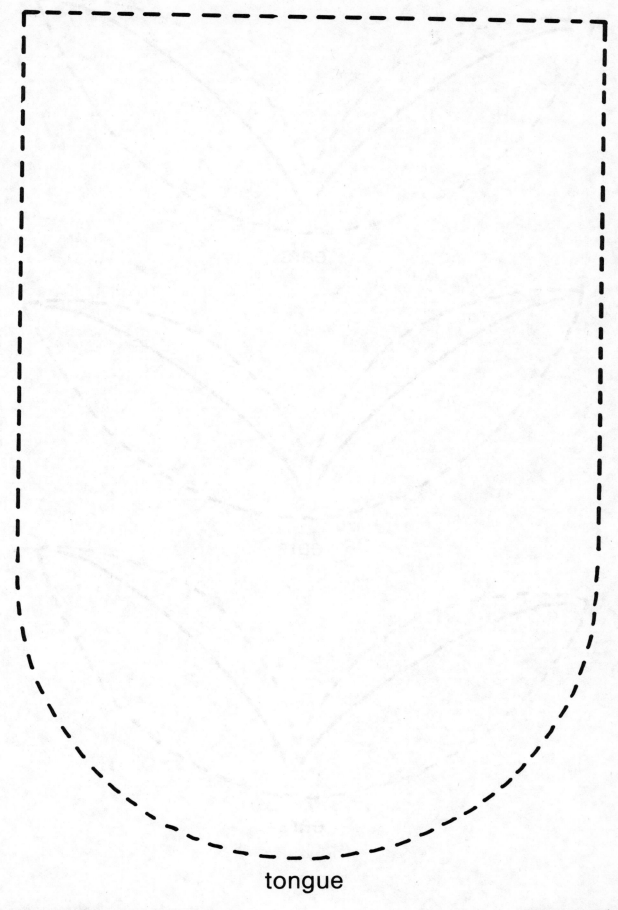

tongue

Pattern C (red)

Hippo 73

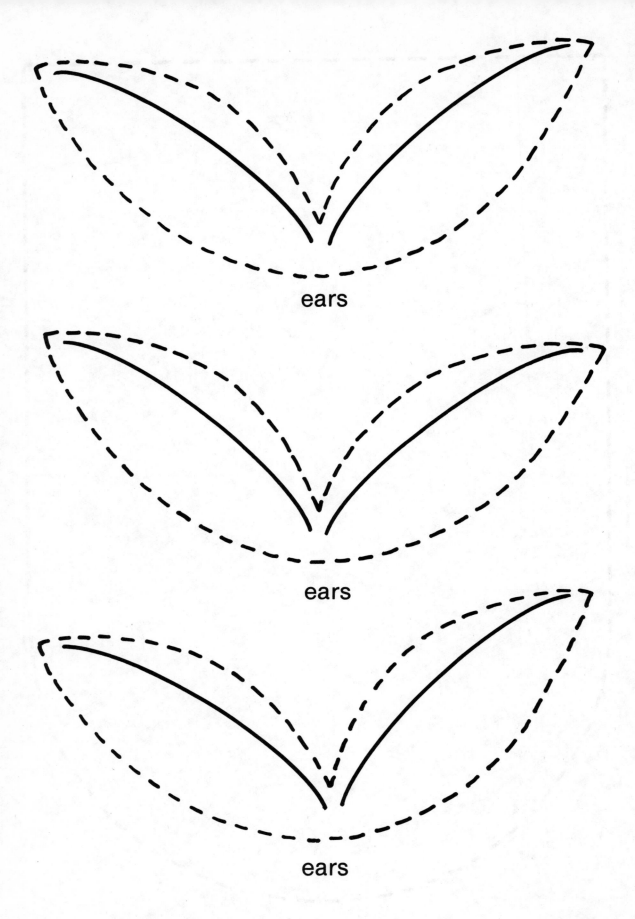

ears

ears

ears

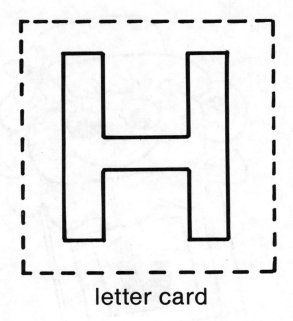

letter card

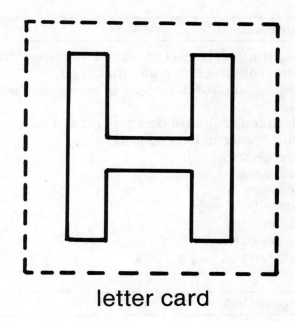

letter card

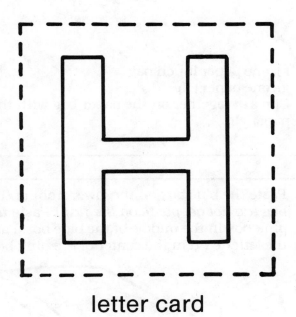

letter card

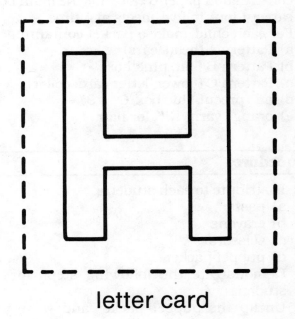

letter card

Pattern E (white)

Jack-in-the-Box

Materials: ☆

- paper lunch bags (11″ × 5¾″) for puppet base
- pink construction paper (hat, box)
- yellow construction paper (flower, collar, letter card)
- flesh tone construction paper (head, ears)
- blue construction paper (box)
- orange yarn (hair)
- crayons
- scissors
- paste
- paper clips
- paper cutter
- patterns on pages 78–80

Preparation: ☆

1. Duplicate patterns on the appropriate colored construction paper.
2. Using a paper cutter, cut sheets of blue construction paper 6″ × 9″ for the main box. You can cut four to five sheets at a time.
3. For each child, make a packet containing:
   a) Pattern A (head, ears)
   b) Pattern B (hat, pink box)
   c) Pattern C (flower, letter card, collar)
   d) one precut blue box, 6″ × 9″
   e) orange yarn, 13″, for hair
   f) one paper lunch bag
   g) one paper clip
   Clip a–e together on the paper bag with the paper clip.

Procedure: ☆

1. Distribute to each student:
   a) paste
   b) crayons
   c) scissors
   d) puppet packet
   Demonstrate the following steps for the students.
2. Unclip the puppet packet and write your name on the back side of the paper lunch bag. Place the bag aside for now.
3. With black crayon, color in the letter *J* on the letter card. Also outline the line in the hat and the flower. Color the center of the flower green.
4. Cut all duplicated patterns along the dotted lines.
5. Paste the blue box on the lower front of the bag (*do not get paste on the flap*). Paste the pink box in the middle of the blue box. Paste the letter card in the center of the pink box.

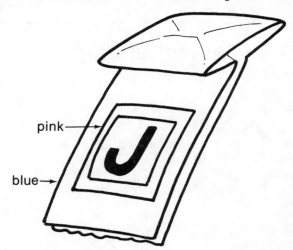

pink→
blue→

6. Run paste along the top edge of the head. Place the hat on the pasted edge. Paste the flower on the side of the hat.

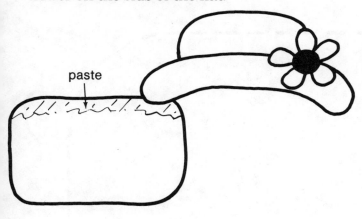

paste

7. Run paste along the side of each ear. Attach the ears below the hat, on the back side of the head.

8. With crayons, add the facial features. With white crayon, color two large ovals for the eyes. Outline the eyes with black crayon. Add pupils and lashes. Add the nose. With red crayon, add the mouth. Draw pink cheeks.

9. Run paste along the top of the collar. Place the head on top of the collar.
10. Paste orange yarn hair along the rim of the hat. Pieces may be cut for variation.

11. Apply paste to the outside edge of the flap.

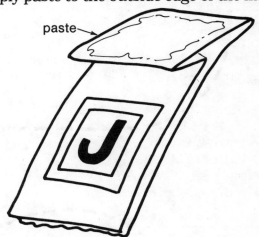

paste

12. Place the head on the pasted flap.
13. Let the puppet dry before using.

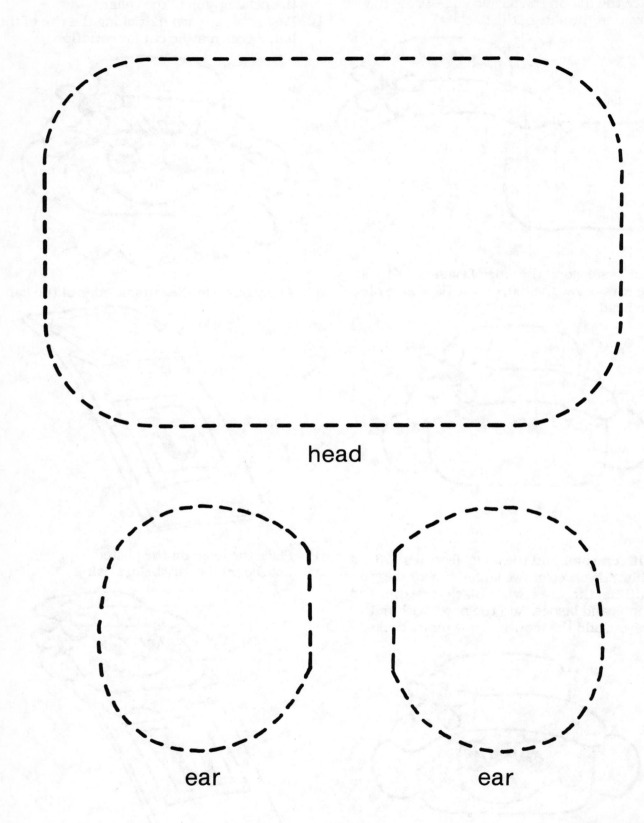

head

ear

ear

Pattern A (flesh tone)

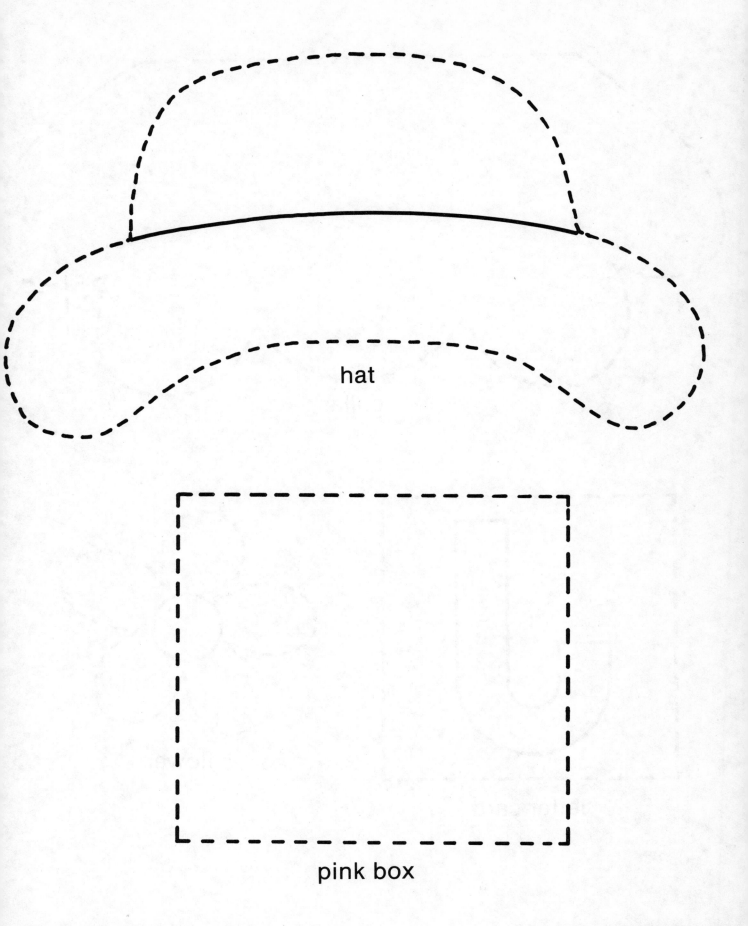

hat

pink box

Pattern B (pink)

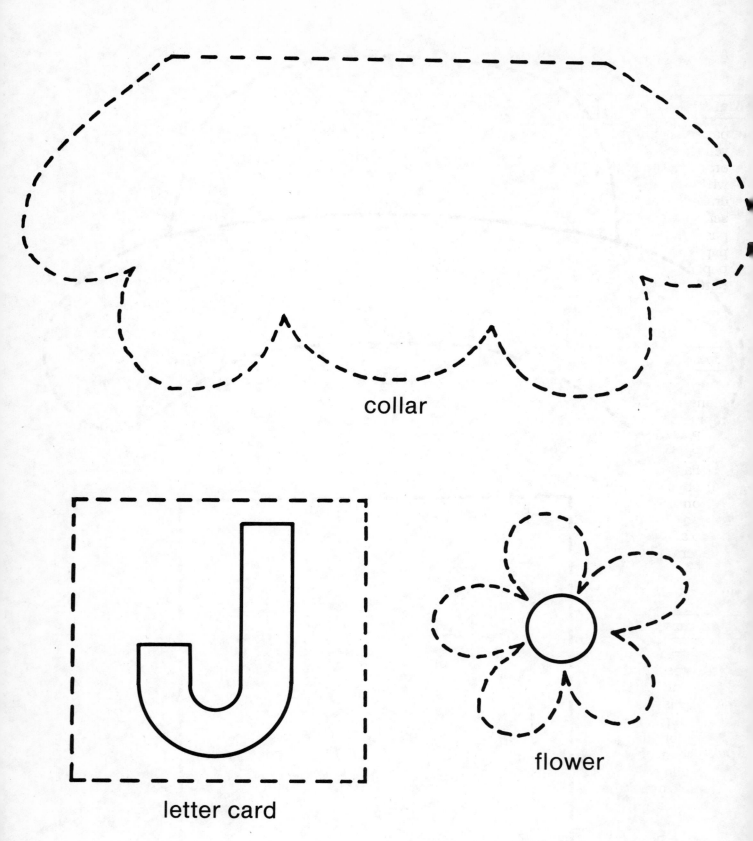

collar

letter card

flower

Lionel Lion

Materials:

- paper lunch bags (11" × 5¾") for puppet base
- yellow construction paper (body, tail, head, ears)
- orange construction paper (mane)
- white construction paper (letter card)
- crayons
- scissors
- paste
- paper clips
- paper cutter
- patterns on pages 83–86

Preparation:

1. Duplicate patterns on the appropriate colored construction paper.
2. For each child, make a packet containing:
   a) Pattern A (body)
   b) Pattern B (head, ears, tail)
   c) Pattern C (mane)
   d) one letter card from Pattern D
   e) one paper lunch bag
   f) one paper clip
   Clip a–d together on the paper bag with the paper clip.

Procedure: ☆

1. Distribute to each student:
   a) paste
   b) crayons
   c) scissors
   d) puppet packet
   Demonstrate the following steps for the students.
2. Unclip the puppet packet and write your name on the back side of the paper lunch bag. Place the bag aside for now.
3. With black crayon, outline the interior lines of the head, feet, and tail. Color the nose black. Color the letter *L* in the letter card black.
4. Cut all duplicated patterns along the dotted lines.

5. With one finger, put paste on the outside edge of the bag (*do not get paste on the flap*). Place the body on the pasted edge and smooth down.

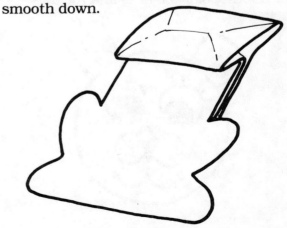

6. Paste the letter card on the lower part of the body.

7. Run paste along the straight edge of each ear. Paste the ears behind the head.

8. With crayons, add the facial features. With white crayon, color two large ovals for the eyes. Outline the eyes with black. Add pupils and lashes. Color the nose and the dots black.

9. Spread paste around the back of the head. Attach the head to the mane.

10. Apply paste to the outside edge of the flap.

paste →

11. Place the head on the pasted flap and smooth down.
12. Paste the tail to the back of the left leg.
13. Let the puppet dry before using.

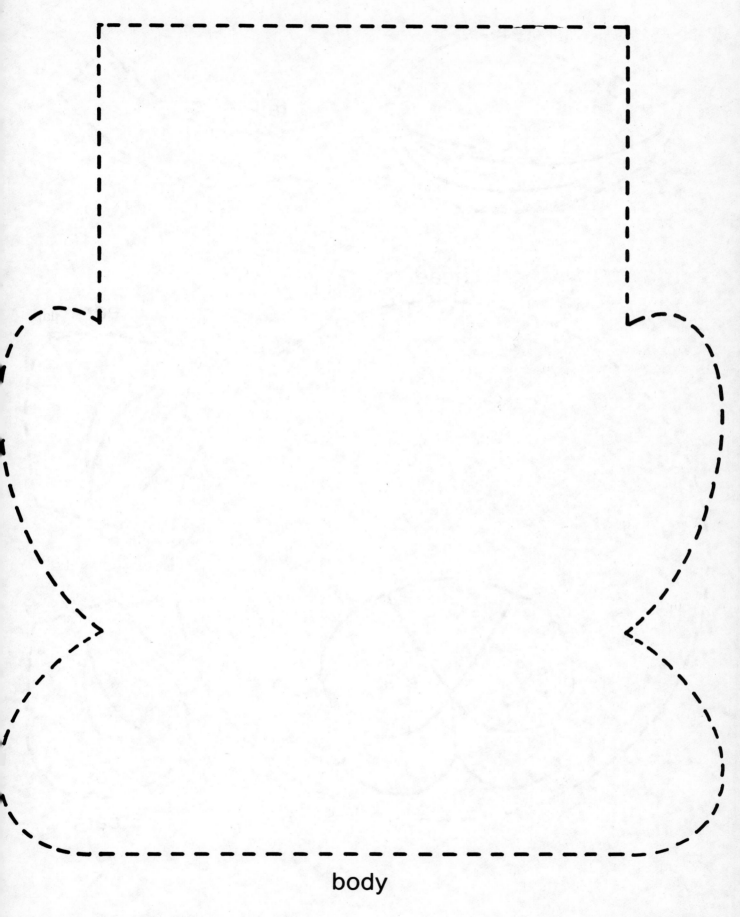

body

Pattern A (yellow)

Lion 83

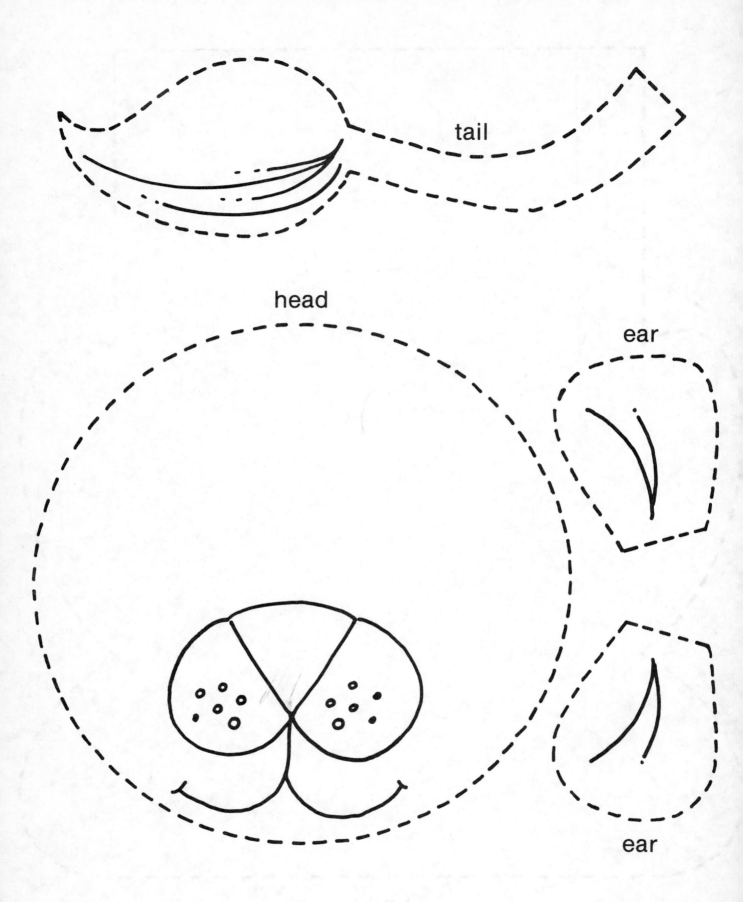

tail

head

ear

ear

mane

Pattern C (orange)

letter card   letter card   letter card

letter card   letter card   letter card

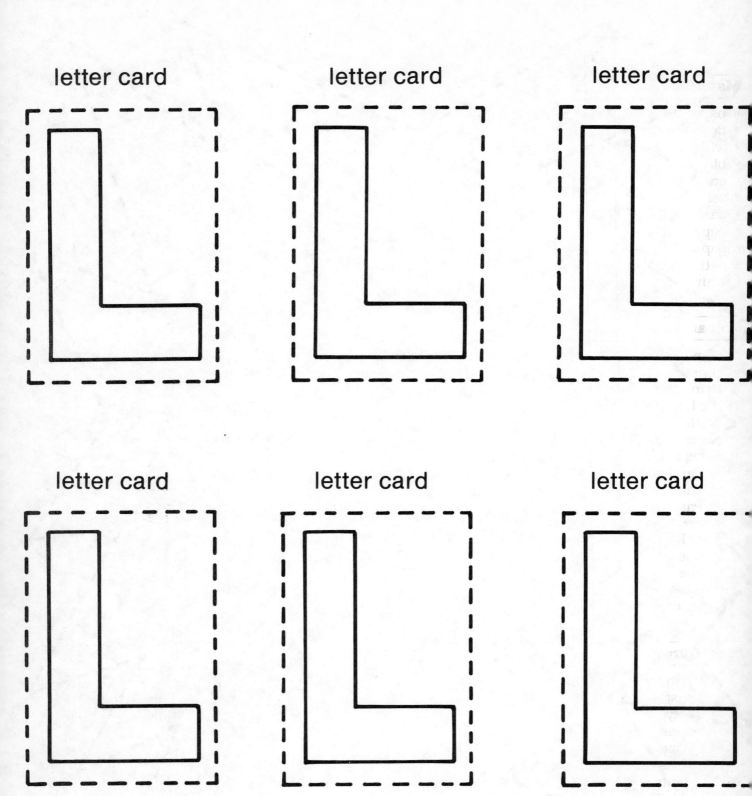

Pattern D (white)

Bagging It with Puppets! © 1988 David S. Lake Publishers

Nurse Nancy or Nurse Ned

Materials:

- paper lunch bags (11″ × 5¾″) for puppet base
- flesh tone construction paper (head, hands)
- white construction paper (uniform, arms, hat)
- black construction paper (hair)
- crayons
- scissors
- paste
- paper clips
- paper cutter
- patterns on pages 89–93
- white china marker or pencil

Preparation:

1. Duplicate patterns on the appropriate colored construction paper.
2. Using the white china marker or pencil, trace the hair pattern for Nurse Ned *or* Nurse Nancy (Pattern E *or* Pattern D) on black construction paper. Make one hair pattern for each puppet.
3. For each child, make a packet containing:
   a) Pattern A (uniform)
   b) Pattern B (hat, arms)
   c) Pattern C (head, hands)
   d) pretraced Pattern D (Nurse Nancy's hair) *or* Pattern E (Nurse Ned's hair)
   e) one paper lunch bag
   f) one paper clip
   Clip a–d together on the paper bag with the paper clip.

Procedure:

1. Distribute to each student:
   a) paste
   b) crayons
   c) scissors
   d) puppet packet
   Demonstrate the following steps for the students.
2. Unclip the puppet packet and write your name on the back side of the paper lunch bag. Place the bag aside for now.
3. With black crayon, outline the interior lines of the uniform and color in the buttons.
4. With red crayon, color in the cross on the hat and the letter *N* on the pocket.
5. Cut all duplicated and pretraced patterns along the dotted lines.

6. With one finger, put paste on the outside edge of the bag (*do not get paste on the flap*). Place the uniform on the pasted edge. Smooth down.

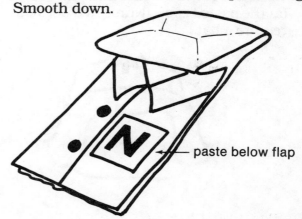

paste below flap

7. Run paste along the inside edge of each arm. Attach the arms below the flap, in the creases of the bag.

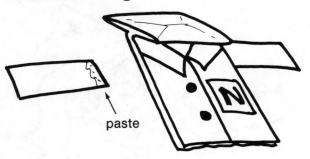

paste

8. Paste the hands, thumbs up, behind the arms.

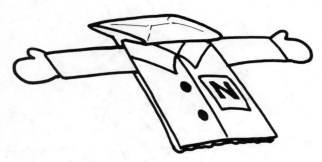

9. Run paste along the top and sides of the head. Place the hair (Pattern D *or* Pattern E) on the pasted edges.

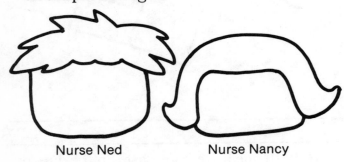

Nurse Ned   Nurse Nancy

10. If you are making Nurse Nancy, run paste along the top of the hair and place the hat on the pasted edge. (Nurse Ned does not require a hat.)

11. With crayons, add the facial features. With white crayon, draw two large ovals for the eyes. Outline the eyes with black and add pupils and lashes. Add the nose. With red crayon, add the mouth. Add cheeks with pink crayon.

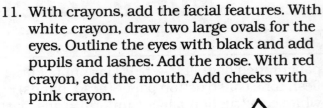

12. Apply paste to the outside edge of the flap.

paste

13. Place the head on the pasted flap.
14. Let the puppet dry before using.

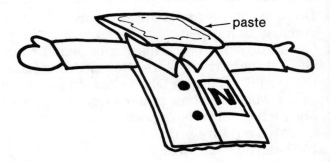

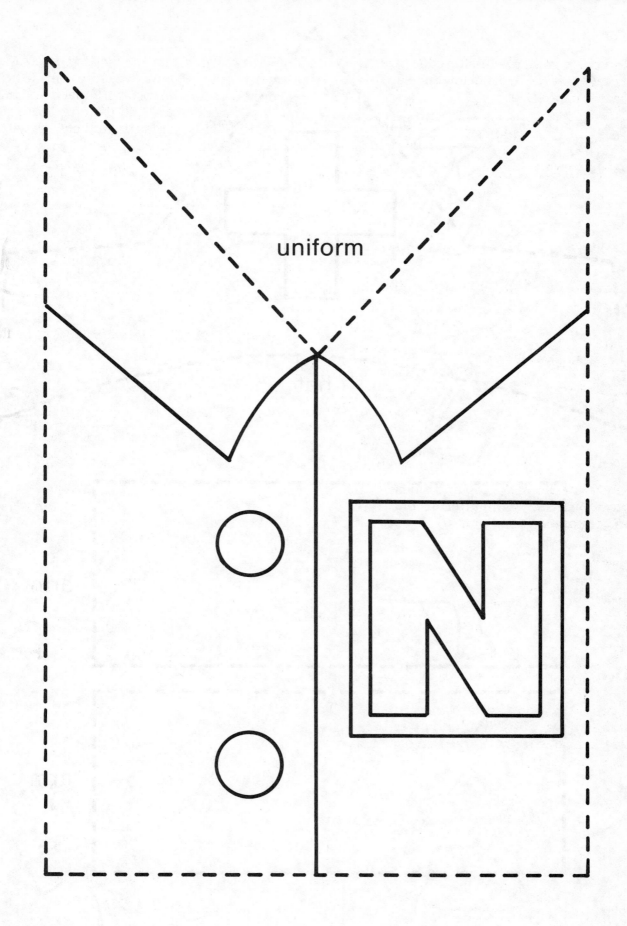

uniform

N

Pattern A (white)

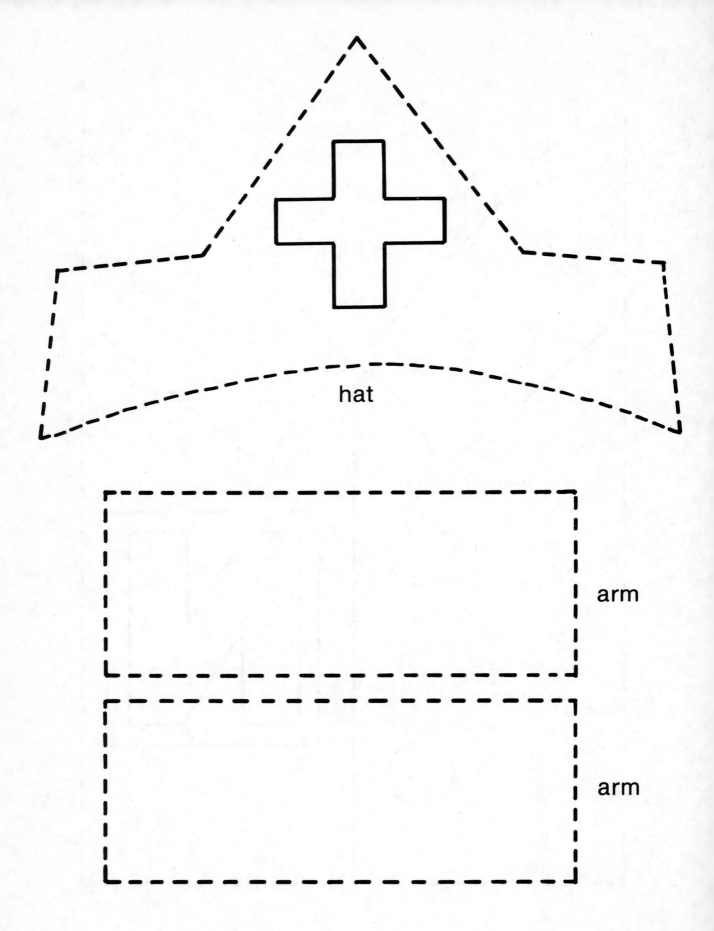

hat

arm

arm

Pattern B (white)

Bagging It with Puppets! © 1988 David S. Lake Publishers

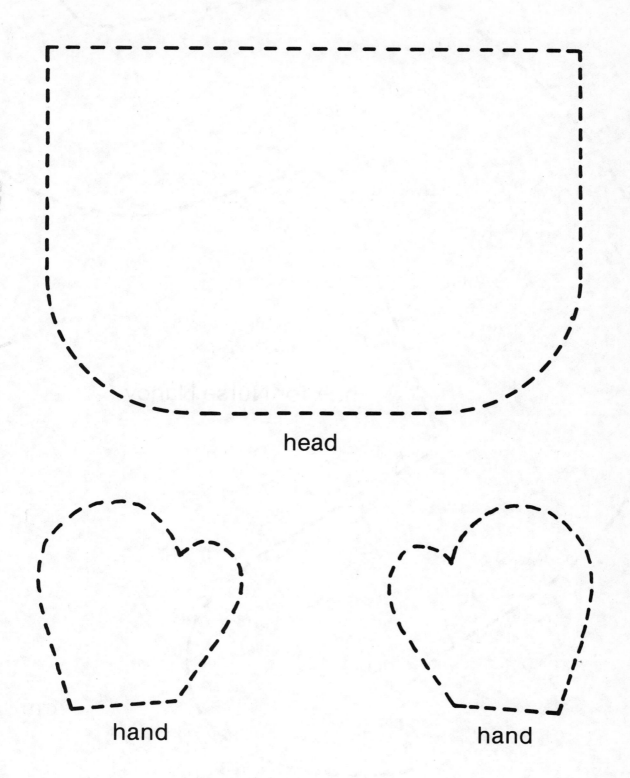

head

hand

hand

Pattern C (flesh tone)

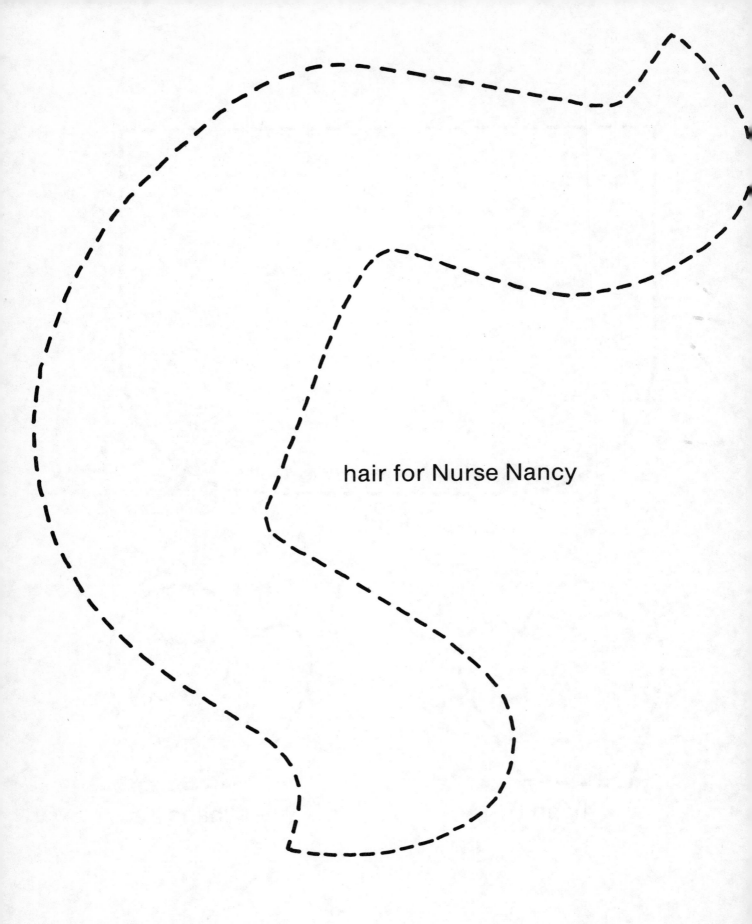

hair for Nurse Nancy

Pattern D (black)

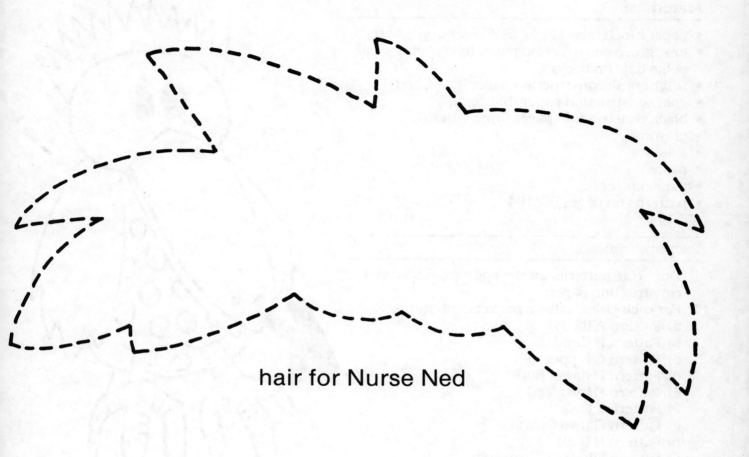

hair for Nurse Ned

Pattern E (black)

Kooky Kookaburra

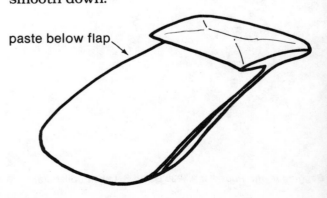

Materials: ☆

- paper lunch bags (11″ × 5¾″) for puppet base
- lime green construction paper (crest, wings, tail, polka dots on body)
- bright pink construction paper (head, body)
- gold construction paper (bill, feet)
- black construction paper (eyes, letter *K*)
- crayons
- scissors
- paste
- paper cutter
- patterns on pages 96–104

Preparation: ☆

1. Duplicate patterns on the appropriate colored construction paper.
2. For each child, make a packet containing:
   a) Pattern A (body)
   b) Pattern B (head)
   c) Pattern C (upper bill)
   d) Pattern D (lower bill)
   e) Pattern E (two feet)
   f) Pattern F (crest)
   g) Pattern G (two wings)
   h) Pattern H (tail)
   i) Pattern I (letter *K*, two eyes)
   j) one sheet of lime green construction paper for polka dots
   k) one paper lunch bag
   l) one paper clip
   Clip a–j together on the paper bag with the paper clip.

Procedure: ☆

1. Distribute to each student:
   a) paste
   b) crayons
   c) scissors
   d) puppet packet
   Demonstrate the following steps for the students.
2. Unclip the puppet packet and write your name on the back of the paper lunch bag. Place the bag aside for now.
3. With black crayon, outline the head, wings, bill, crest, feet, tail, and body. Fill in the nostrils on the upper bill with black crayon.
4. Cut all duplicated patterns along the dotted lines.

5. With one finger, put paste on the outside edge of the bag (*do not get paste on the flap*). Place the body on the pasted edge and smooth down.

paste below flap

6. Apply paste to the outside edge of the flap. Place the head on the pasted flap. Smooth down.

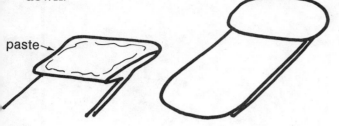

paste

7. Apply paste to the lower edge of the crest. Attach the crest to the back of the head. Smooth down.

paste

8. Paste the wings to the body.

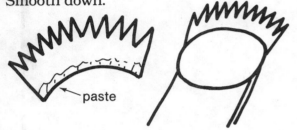

9. Paste the feet to the bottom of the body. With black crayon, draw half a circle where each foot meets the body.

10. Paste the tail to the back of the bag.

11. Cut out lime green polka dots and paste them to the body.

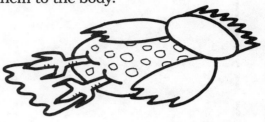

12. Prepare the bill by cutting and folding as indicated on the patterns. Place the upper bill over the lower bill and paste them together as shown.

cut
fold

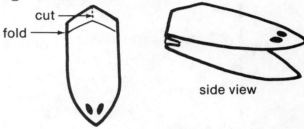

side view

13. Attach the bill to the head with paste.

14. Paste the eyes on the head, above the bill.

15. Paste the letter *K* to the edge of the lower bill.
16. Let the puppet dry before using.

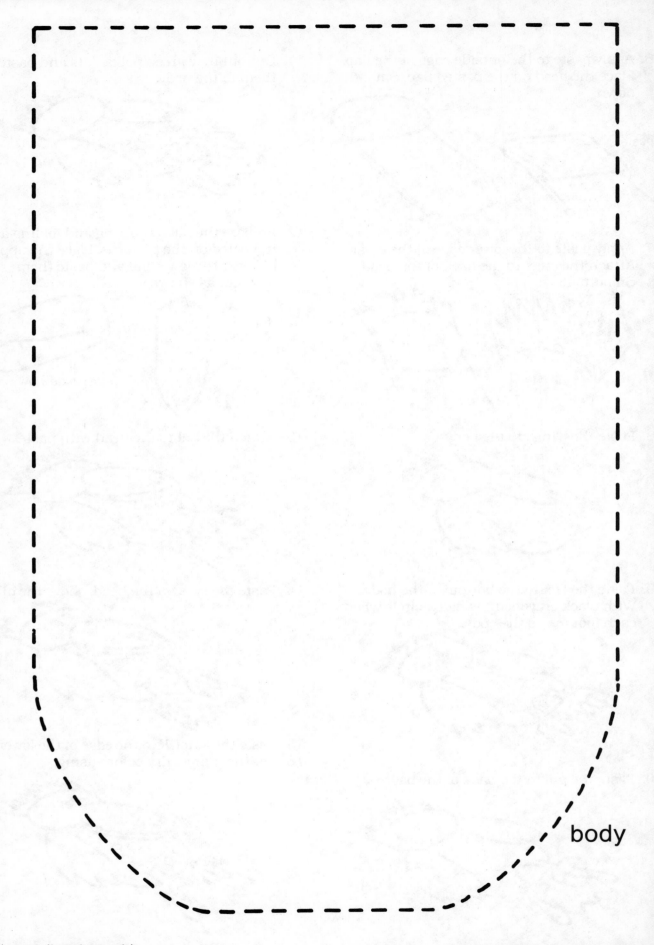

body

Pattern A (bright pink)

96 Kooky

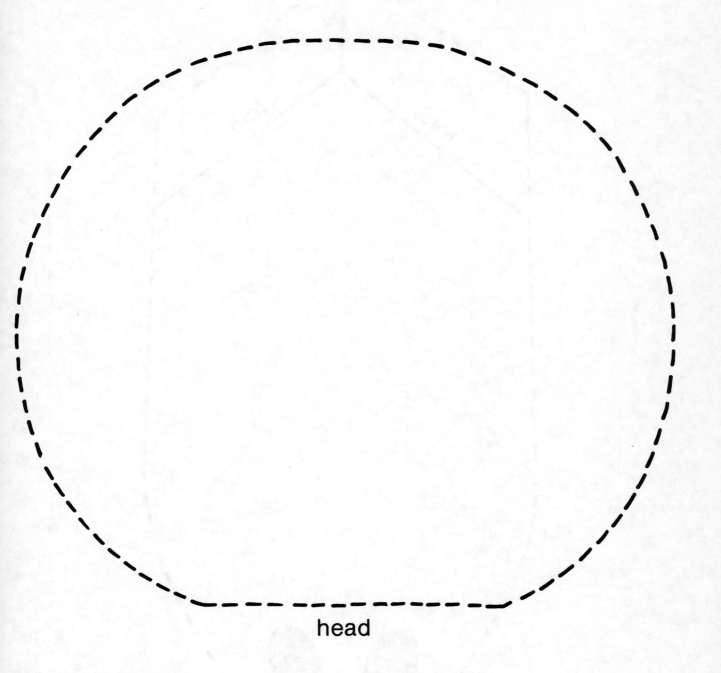

head

Pattern B (bright pink)

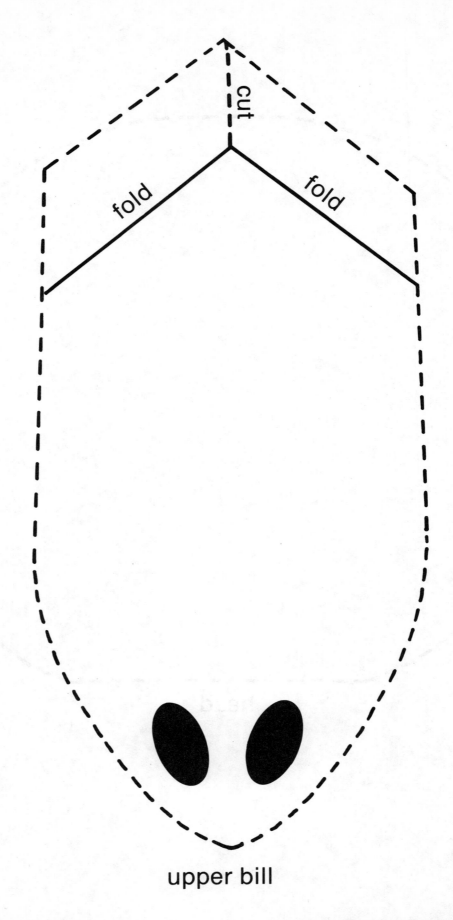

upper bill

Pattern C (gold)

98 Kooky

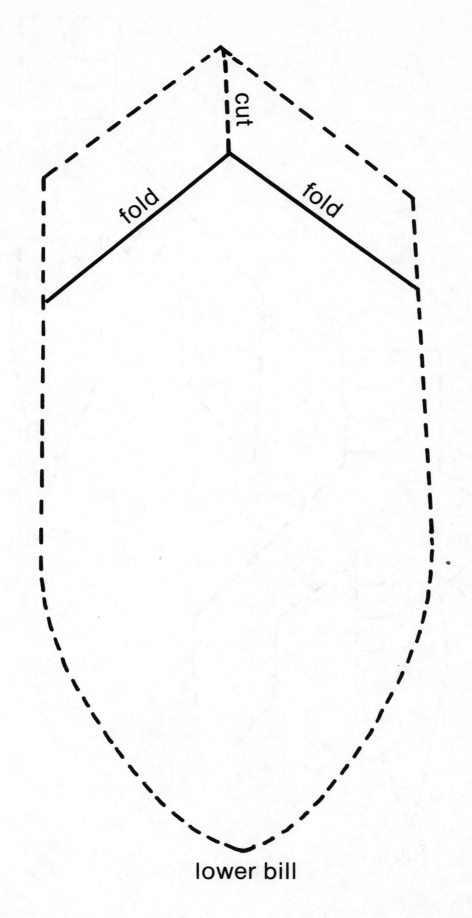

cut

fold

fold

lower bill

Pattern D (gold)

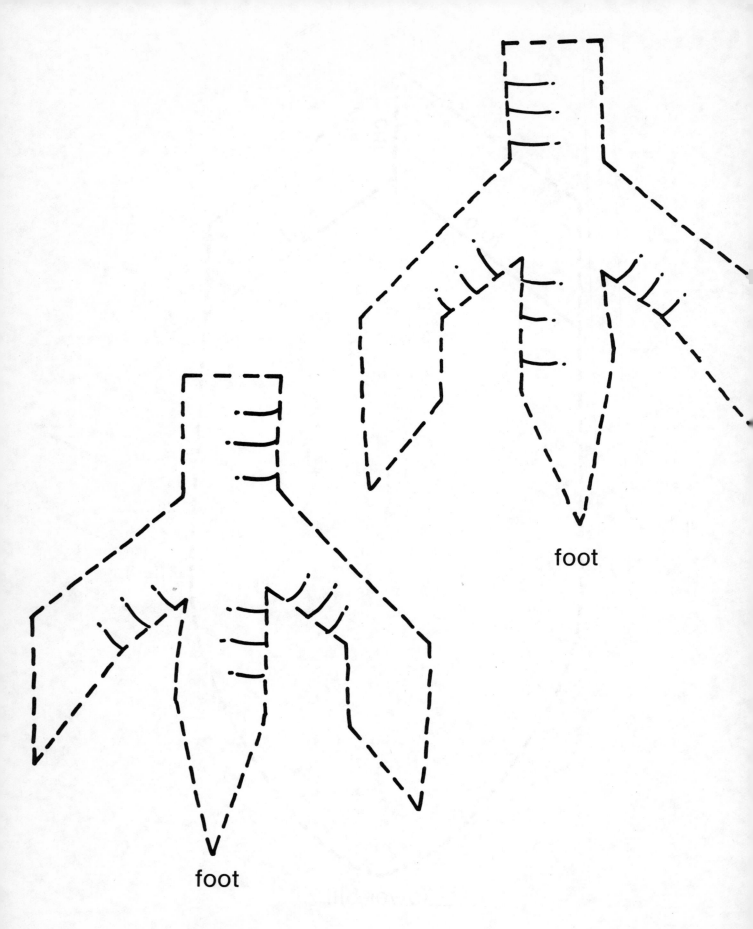

foot

foot

Pattern E (gold)

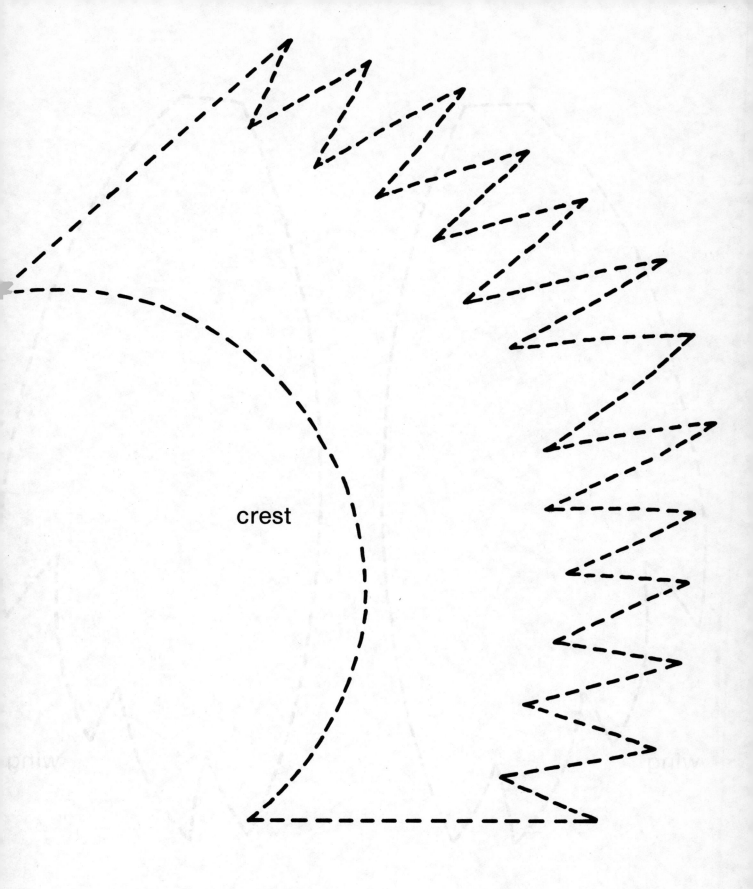

crest

Pattern F (lime green)

Kooky 101

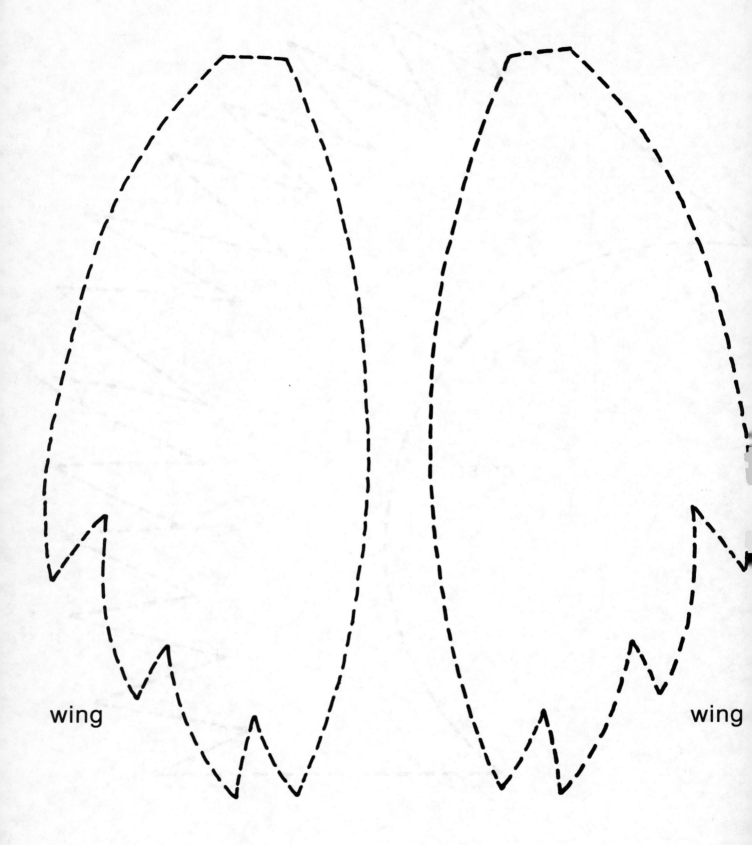

wing

wing

Pattern G (lime green)

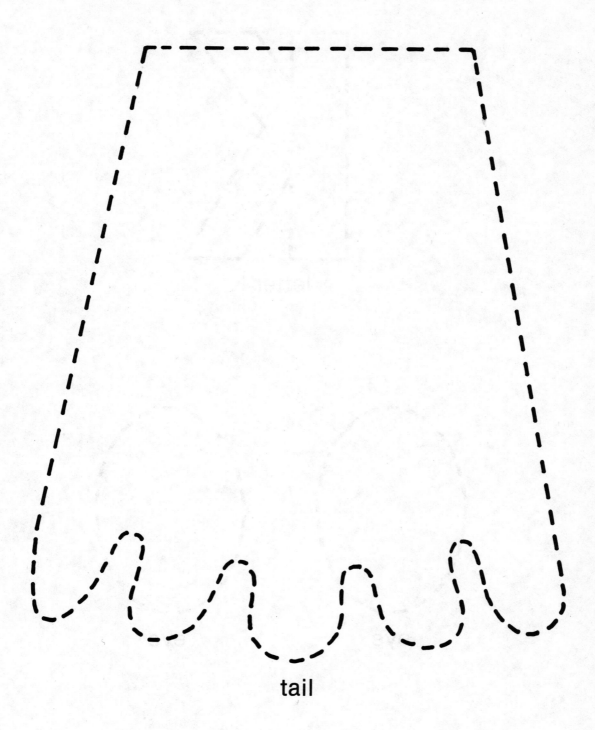

tail

Pattern H (lime green)

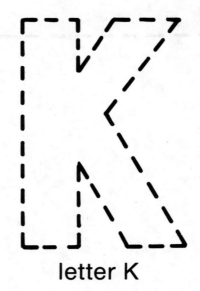

letter K

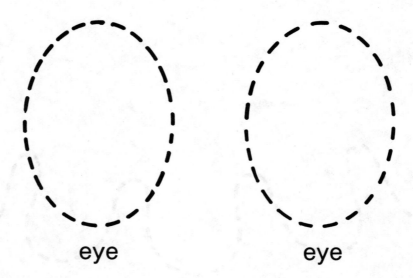

eye   eye

Bagging It with Puppets! © 1988 David S. Lake Publishers

Peter Pig

Materials: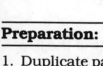

- paper lunch bags (11″ × 5¾″) for puppet base
- yellow construction paper (shirt, sleeves)
- pink construction paper (head, hooves)
- light blue construction paper (bow tie)
- crayons
- scissors
- paste
- paper clips
- paper cutter
- patterns on pages 107–109

Preparation: ☆

1. Duplicate patterns on the appropriate colored construction paper.
2. For each child, make a packet containing:
   a) Pattern A (head, hooves)
   b) Pattern B (shirt, sleeves)
   c) one bow tie from Pattern C
   d) one paper lunch bag
   e) one paper clip
   Clip a–c together on the paper bag with the paper clip.

Procedure: ☆

1. Distribute to each student:
   a) paste
   b) crayons
   c) scissors
   d) puppet packet
   Demonstrate the following steps for the students.
2. Unclip the puppet packet and write your name on the back side of the paper lunch bag. Place the bag aside for now.
3. With black crayon, outline the interior lines of the patterns. Color in the letter *P* on the shirt with black crayon. Color the hooves black. Color the pupils black and the rest of the eyes white. With red crayon, color in the polka dots on the bow tie; outline them with black crayon. Add a big smile to the face with red crayon.

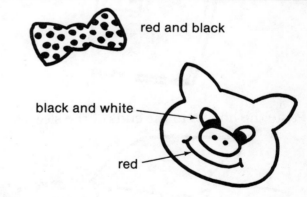

red and black

black and white

red

4. Cut all duplicated patterns along the dotted lines.

black

black

5. With one finger, put paste on the outside edge of the bag *(do not get paste on the flap)*. Place the shirt on the pasted edge and smooth down.

paste below flap

6. Run paste along the inside edge of each sleeve. Attach the sleeves below the flap, in the creases of the bag.

7. Paste the hooves to the ends of the sleeves.

8. Paste the bow tie to the shirt.

9. Apply paste to the outside edge of the flap.

paste

10. Place the head on the pasted flap.
11. Let the puppet dry before using.

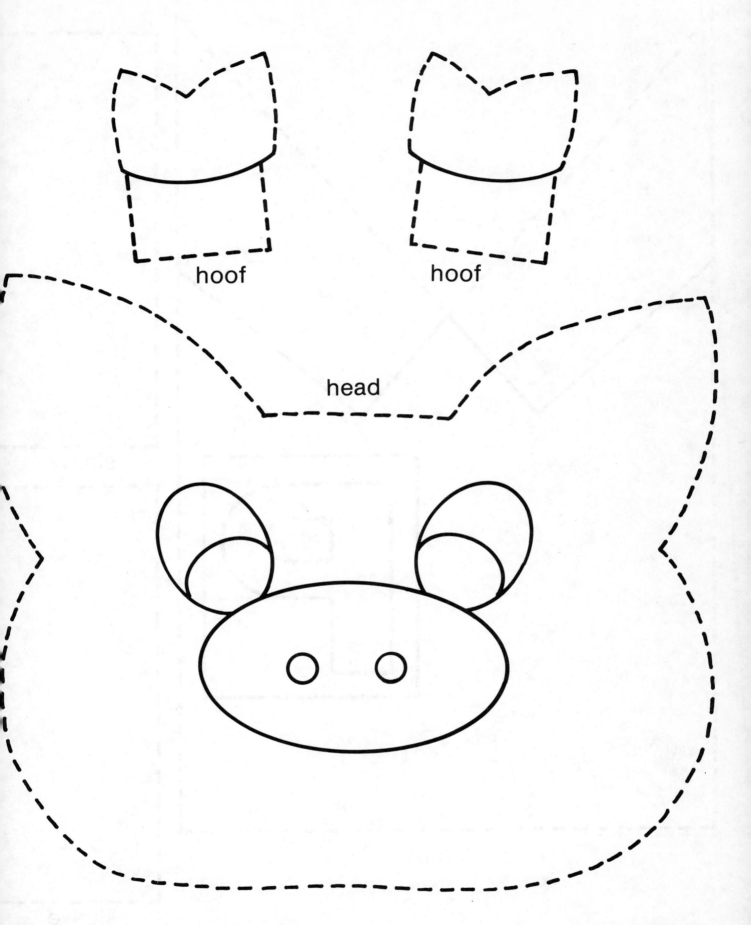

hoof

hoof

head

Pattern A (pink)

Pig   107

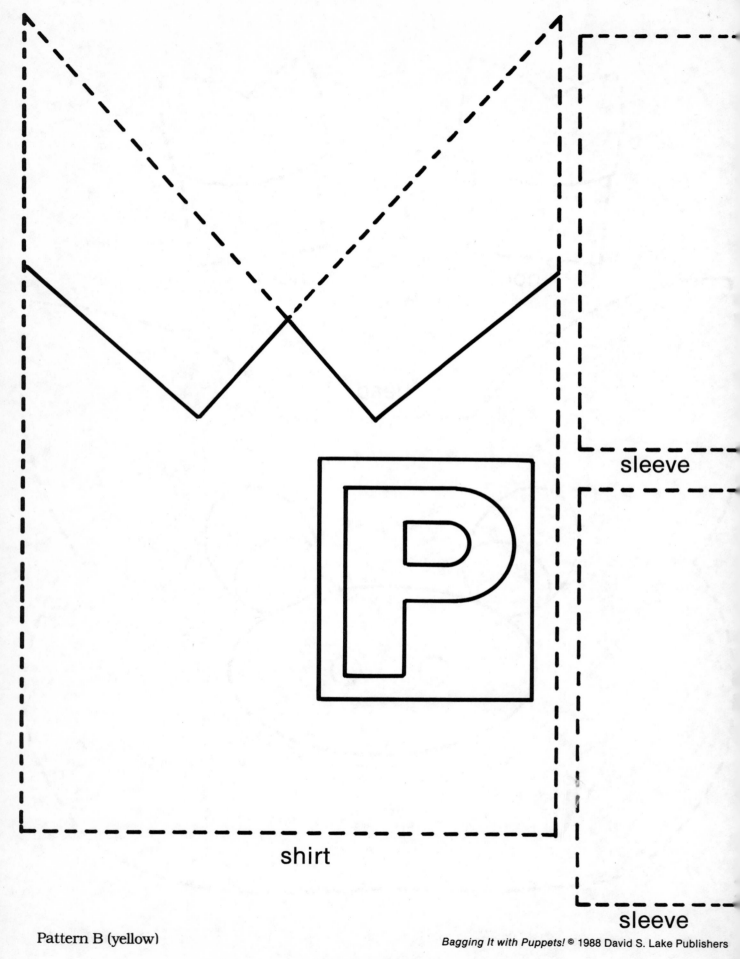

sleeve

sleeve

shirt

Pattern B (yellow)

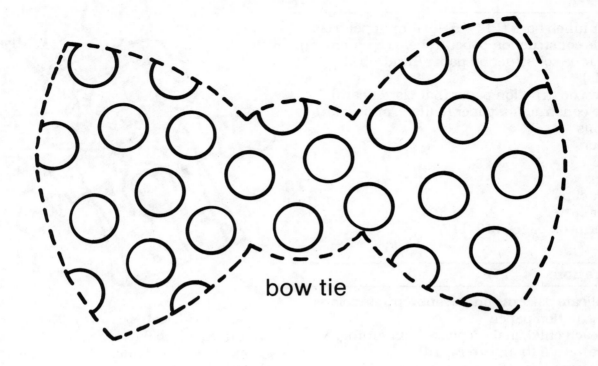

bow tie

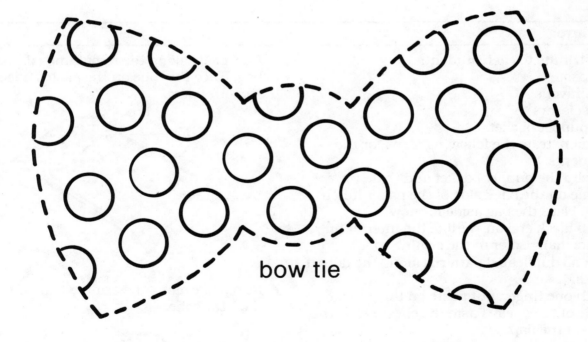

bow tie

Pattern C (light blue)

Queenie Queen

Materials: ☆

- paper lunch bags (11″ × 5¾″) for puppet base
- purple construction paper (robe, sleeves, crown)
- flesh tone construction paper (head, chest, hands)
- yellow construction paper (hair, letter card)
- white construction paper (cuffs, ermine trim)
- crayons
- scissors
- paste
- glitter
- paper clips
- paper cutter
- patterns on pages 112–117

Preparation: ☆

1. Duplicate patterns on the appropriate colored construction paper.
2. For each child, make a packet containing:
   a) Pattern A (hair, letter card)
   b) Pattern B (cuffs, ermine trim)
   c) Pattern C (head)
   d) Pattern D (hands, chest)
   e) Pattern E (sleeves, crown)
   f) Pattern F (robe)
   g) one paper lunch bag
   h) one paper clip
   Clip a–f together on the paper bag with the paper clip.

Procedure: ☆

1. Distribute to each student:
   a) paste
   b) crayons
   c) scissors
   d) puppet packet
   Demonstrate the following steps for the students.
2. Unclip the puppet packet and write your name on the back side of the paper lunch bag. Place the bag aside for now.
3. With black crayon, outline the interior lines of the hair. Color in the ermine spots.
4. Cut all duplicated patterns along the dotted lines.
5. With one finger, put paste on the outside edge of the chest. Paste the chest below the fold of the flap.

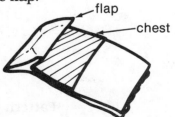

6. Run paste along the remaining edges of the bag. Place the robe on the pasted edges and smooth down.

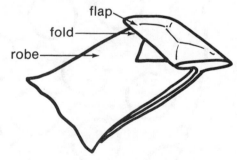

7. Run paste along the ermine trim and place it on the robe.

8. Apply paste to the inside edge of each sleeve. Attach the sleeves below the flap, in the creases of the bag.

9. Paste the cuffs on the ends of the sleeves.

10. Run paste along the inside edge of each hand. Attach the hands behind the sleeves.

11. Run paste along the straight edge of the head. Place the hair on the head.

12. With crayons, add the facial features. With white crayon, make two large ovals for the eyes. Outline the eyes with black. Add pupils and lashes. Add the nose. With red crayon, add the mouth.

13. Apply paste to the outside edge of the flap. Place the head on the pasted flap and smooth down.

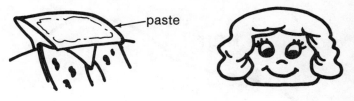

14. Apply paste to the straight edge of the crown. Place the crown on the hair.

15. Decorate the crown with glitter.

16. Make a glitter chain. Paste the letter card at the end of the chain.

17. Let the puppet dry before using.

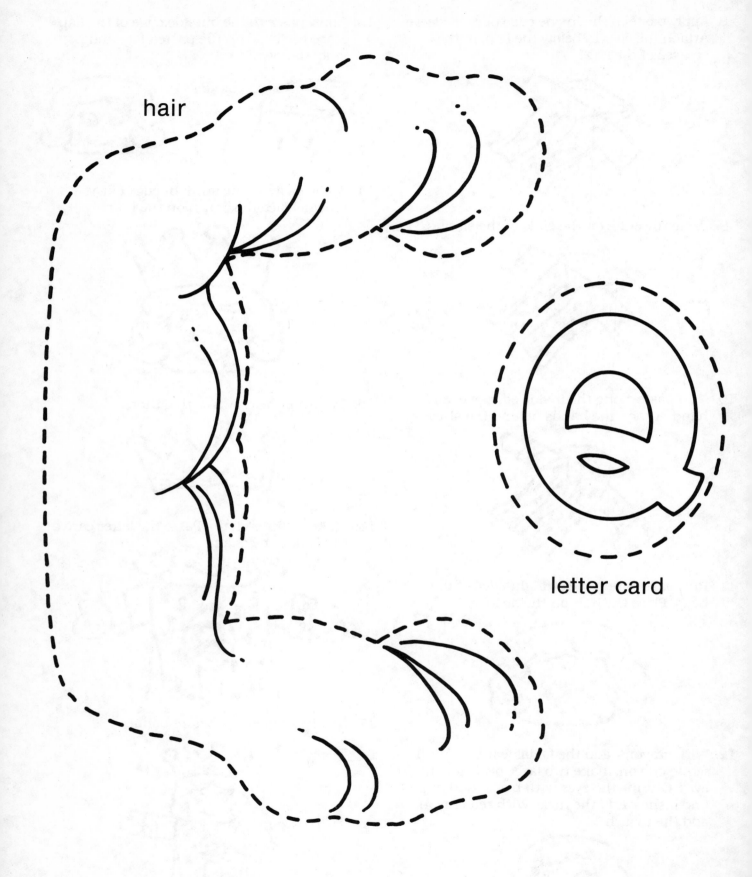

hair

letter card

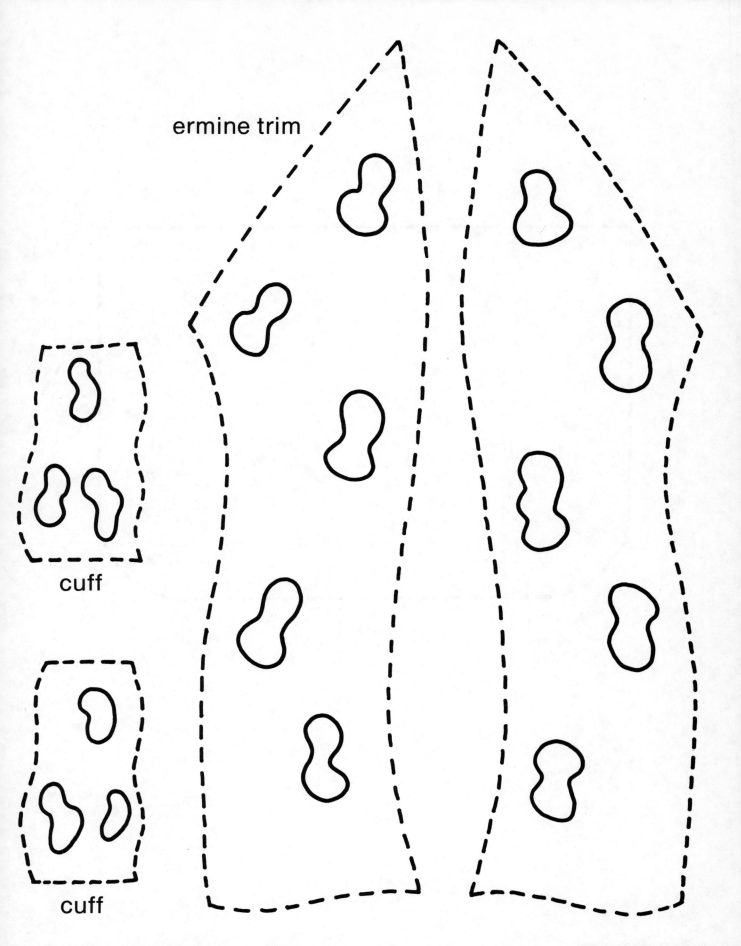

ermine trim

cuff

cuff

Pattern B (white)

Queen 113

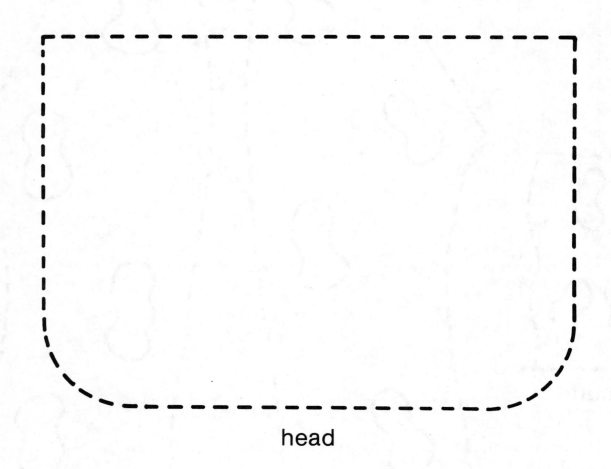

head

Bagging It with Puppets! © 1988 David S. Lake Publishers

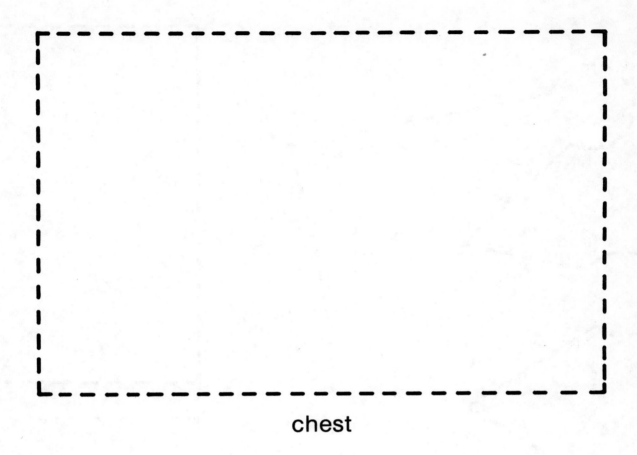

chest

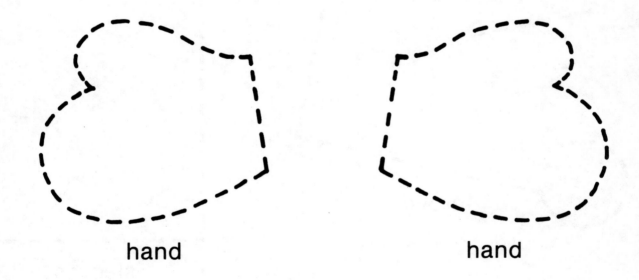

hand   hand

Pattern D (flesh tone)

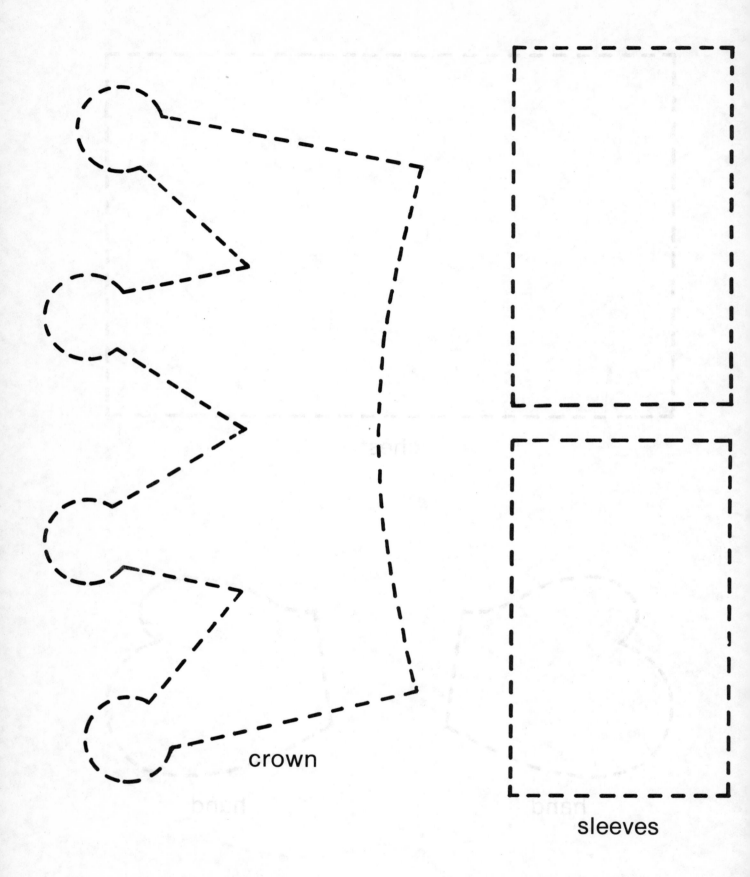

crown

sleeves

Pattern E (purple)

Bagging It with Puppets! © 1988 David S. Lake Publishers

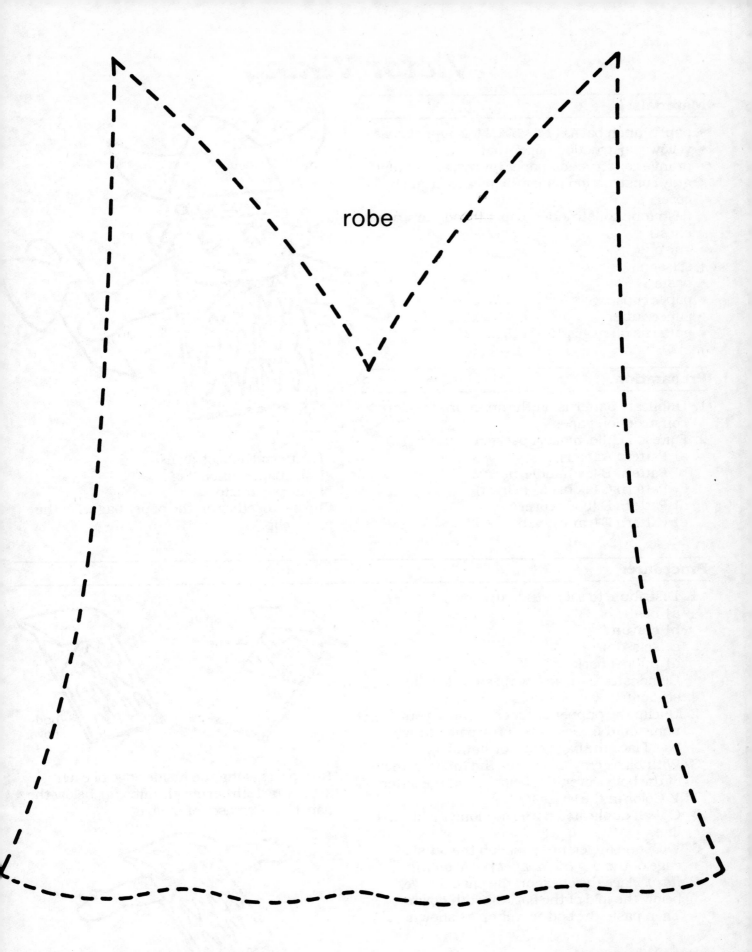

robe

Pattern F (purple)

Victor Viking

Materials: ☆

- paper lunch bags (11″ × 5¾″) for puppet base
- yellow construction paper (hair)
- orange construction paper (horns, ax handle)
- gray construction paper (helmet, ax head, body cover)
- flesh tone construction paper (head, ears, arms, chest)
- crayons
- scissors
- paste
- paper clips
- paper cutter
- patterns on pages 120–125

Preparation: ☆

1. Duplicate patterns on the appropriate colored construction paper.
2. For each child, make a packet containing:
   a) Pattern A (hair)
   b) Pattern B (ax handle, horns)
   c) Pattern C (ax blade, helmet)
   d) Pattern D (body cover)
   e) Pattern E (ears, head)
   f) Pattern F (chest, arms)
   g) one paper lunch bag
   h) one paper clip
   Clip a–f together on the paper bag with the paper clip.

Procedure: ☆

1. Distribute to each student:
   a) paste
   b) crayons
   c) scissors
   d) puppet packet
   Demonstrate the following steps for the students.
2. Unclip the puppet packet and write your name on the back side of the paper lunch bag. Place the bag aside for now.
3. With black crayon, outline the interior lines of the body cover, the helmet, and the letter *V*. Color in the letter *V*.
4. Cut all duplicated patterns along the dotted lines.
5. With one finger, put paste on the outside edge of the bag (*do not get paste on the flap*). Place the chest on the pasted edge, below the fold of the bag. Smooth down. Then paste the body cover on as shown.

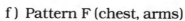
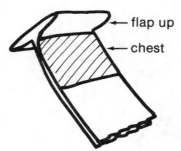
← flap up
← chest
← body cover

6. Run paste along the inside edge of each arm. Attach the arms, thumbs up, below the flap, in the creases of the bag.

7. Run paste along the straight edge of the head. Place the hair on the pasted edge.

8. Apply paste to the lower edge of the helmet (*back side*). Turn the helmet over and attach it to the hair.

9. Run paste along the inside edge of each horn. Paste the horns on the back of the helmet.

10. Apply paste to the straight edge of each ear. Attach the ears below the hair, on each side of the head.

11. With crayons, add the facial features. With white crayon, color two large ovals for the eyes. Outline the eyes with black crayon and add pupils and lashes. Add the nose. With red crayon, add the mouth.

12. Apply paste to the outside edge of the flap. Place the head on the pasted edge. Smooth down.

paste

13. Paste the ax head to the ax handle. Paste the ax to the back of the puppet's hand.

14. Let the puppet dry before using.

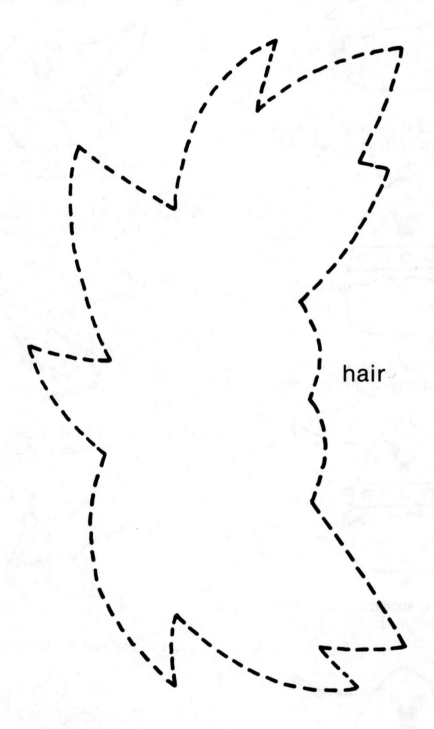

hair

Bagging It with Puppets! © 1988 David S. Lake Publishers

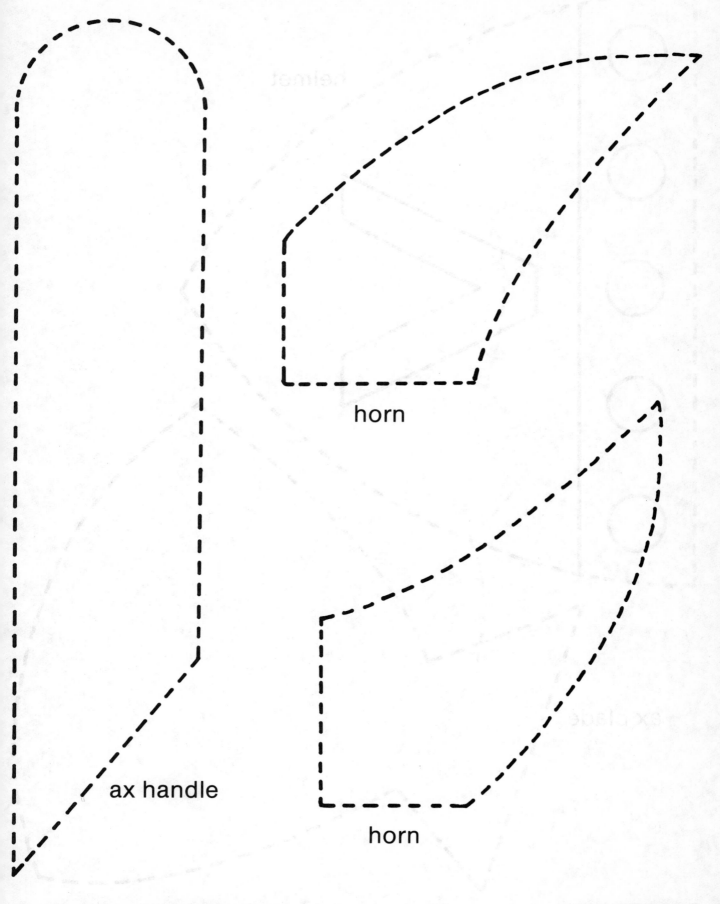

horn

ax handle

horn

Pattern B (orange)

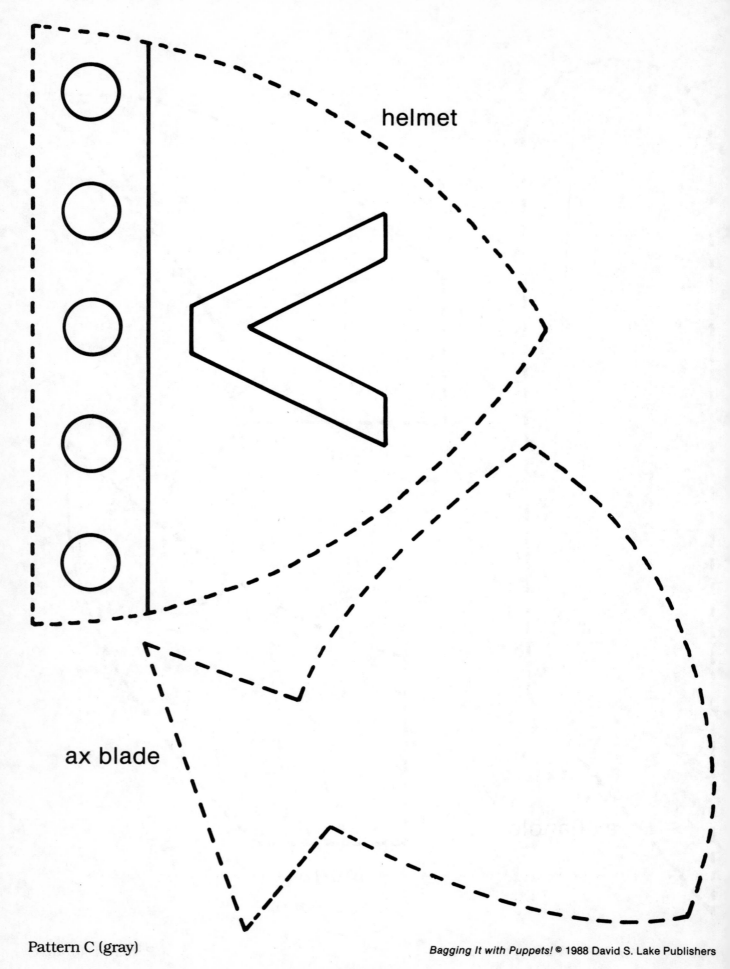

helmet

ax blade

Pattern C (gray)

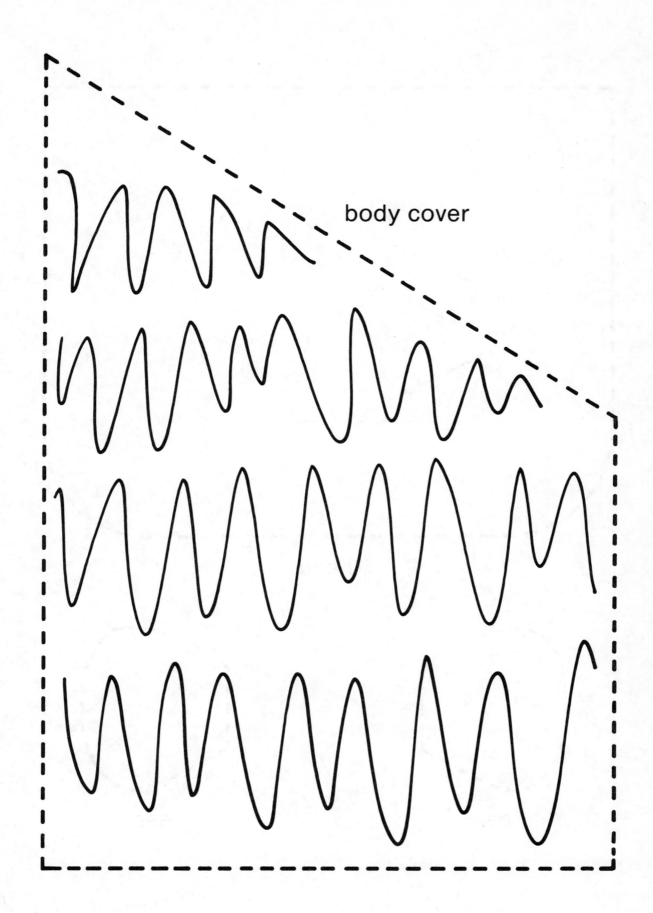

body cover

Pattern D (gray)

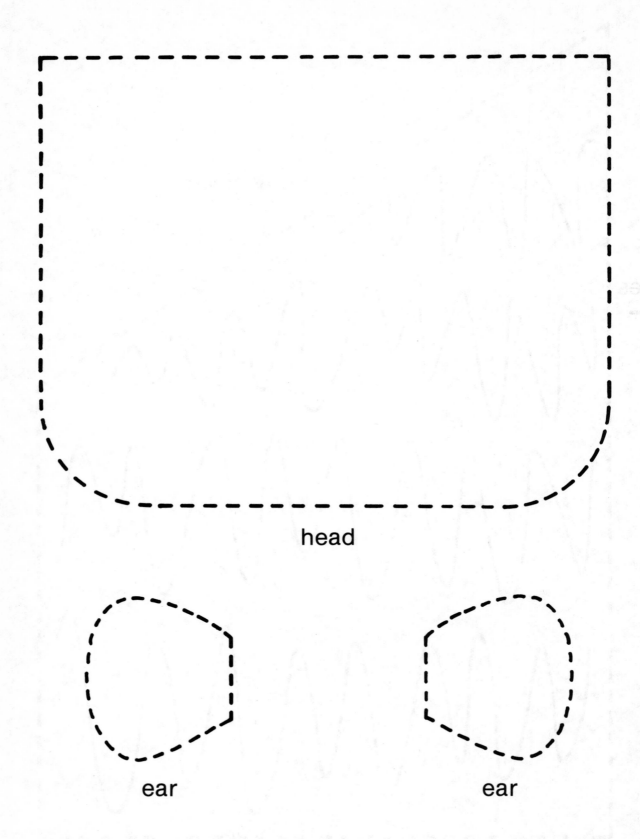

head

ear ear

Pattern E (flesh tone)

124 Victor

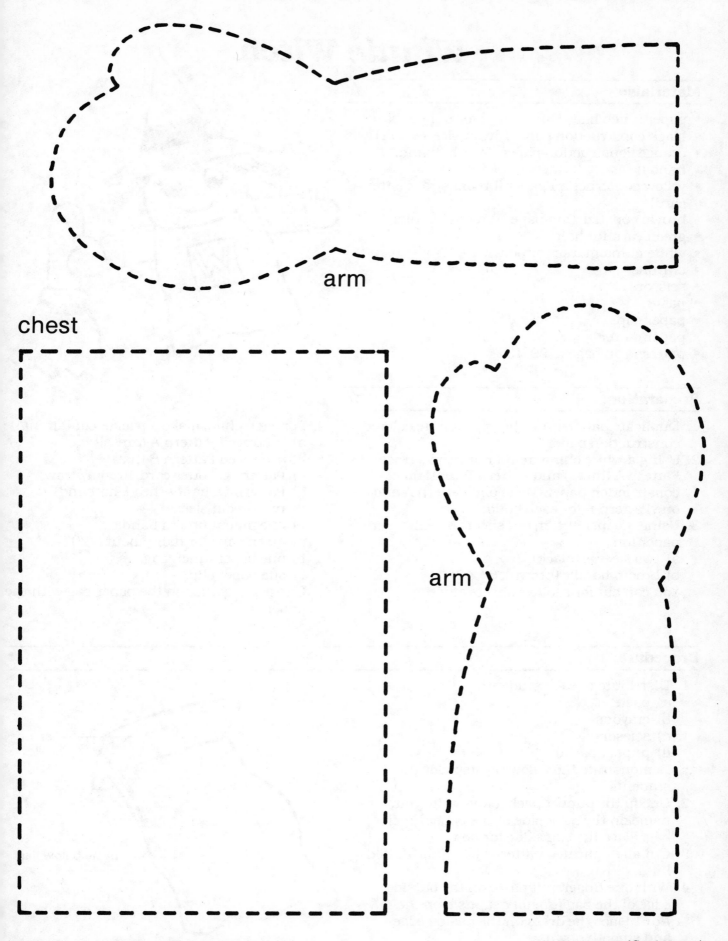

arm

chest

arm

Pattern F (flesh tone)

Winnie Witch

Materials:

- paper lunch bags (11″ × 5¾″) for puppet base
- black construction paper (dress, sleeves, hat)
- orange construction paper (face, hatband, hands)
- yellow construction paper (broom straw, letter card)
- brown construction paper (broom handle)
- green yarn for hair
- white china marker or pencil
- crayons
- scissors
- paste
- paper clips
- paper cutter
- patterns on pages 129–132

Preparation: ☆

1. Duplicate patterns on the appropriate colored construction paper.
2. Using a white china marker or pencil, trace Pattern A (dress) and Pattern B (hat) on black construction paper. Make one Pattern A and one Pattern B for each child.
3. Using a paper cutter, cut sheets of construction paper for:
   a) two sleeves (black), 2″ × 4″
   b) broom handle (brown), 6″ × 2″
   You can cut four to five sheets at a time.

4. For each child, make a packet containing:
   a) pretraced Pattern A (dress)
   b) pretraced Pattern B (hat)
   c) Pattern C (letter card, broom straw)
   d) Pattern D (hands, head, hatband)
   e) two precut sleeves
   f) one precut broom handle
   g) green yarn for hair (about 36″)
   h) one paper lunch bag
   i) one paper clip
   Clip a–g together on the paper bag with the paper clip.

Procedure: ☆

1. Distribute to each student:
   a) paste
   b) crayons
   c) scissors
   d) puppet packet
   Demonstrate the following steps for the students.
2. Unclip the puppet packet and write your name on the back side of the paper lunch bag. Place the bag aside for now.
3. Cut all duplicated patterns along the dotted lines.
4. With one finger, put paste on the outside edge of the bag (*do not get paste on the flap*). Place the dress on the pasted edge and smooth down.

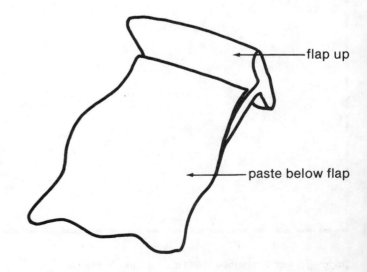

flap up

paste below flap

5. Run paste along the inside edge of each sleeve. Attach the sleeves below the flap, in the creases of the bag.

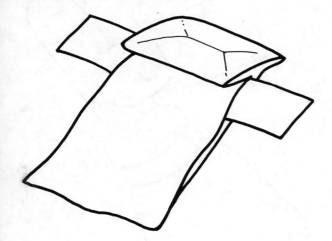

6. Run paste along the inside edge of each hand. Place the hands behind the sleeves.

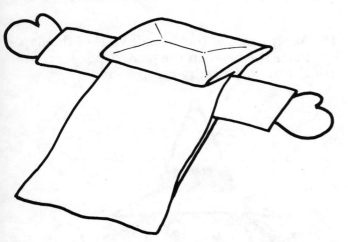

7. Run paste along the straight edge of the head.

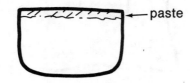
← paste

8. Place three strands of yarn on each side of the head. Place the hat over the hair and the remaining paste.

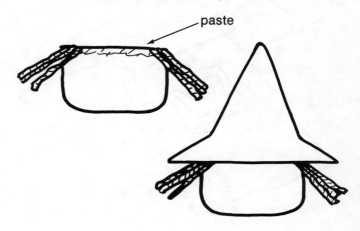
paste

9. With crayons, add the facial features. With white crayon, color two large ovals for the eyes. Outline the eyes with black; add pupils and lashes. Add the nose and the mouth.

10. Apply paste to the hatband. Place the hatband on the hat and trim it to fit the hat.

11. Paste the letter card to the dress.

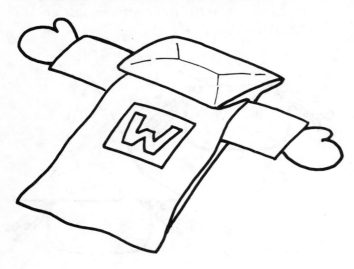

12. With scissors, round one edge of the 6″ x 2″ brown rectangle to form a broom handle.

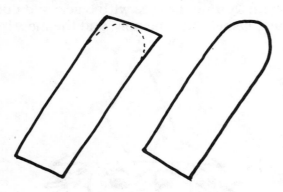

13. Paste the handle of the broom to the back side of the broom straw.

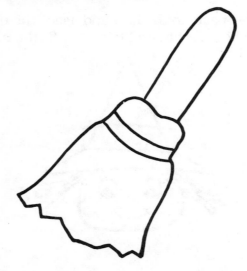

14. Paste the broom handle to the back of one hand.

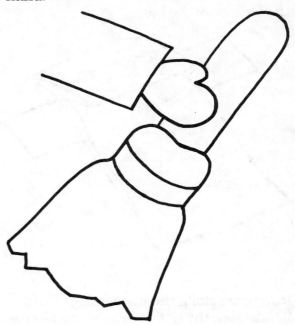

15. Apply paste to the outside edge of the flap. Place the head on the pasted flap.
16. Let the puppet dry before using.

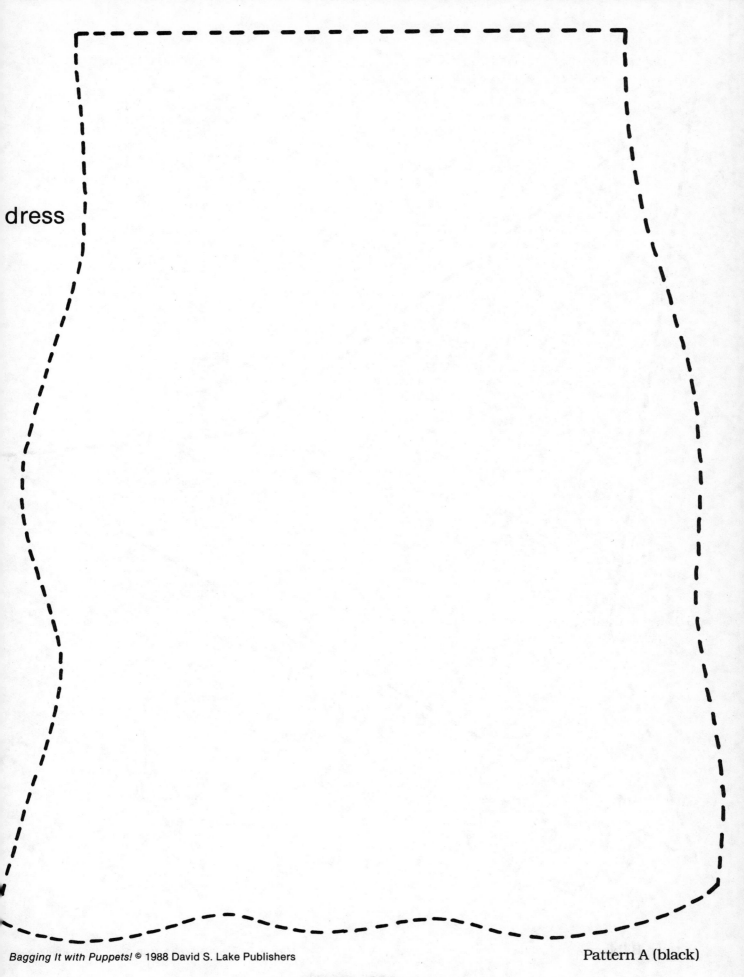

dress

Pattern A (black)

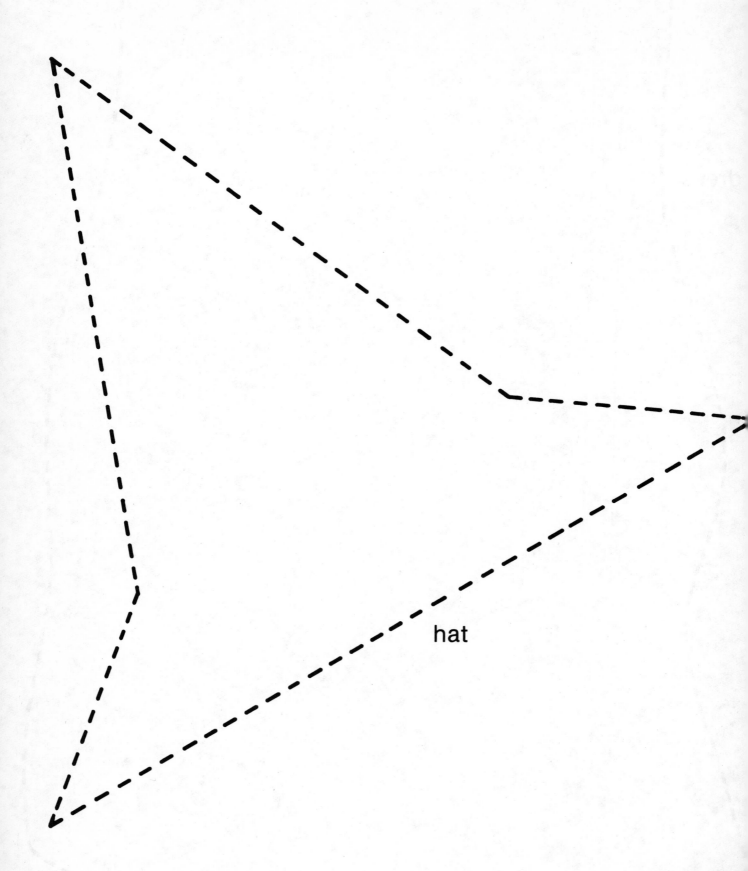

hat

Pattern B (black)

letter card

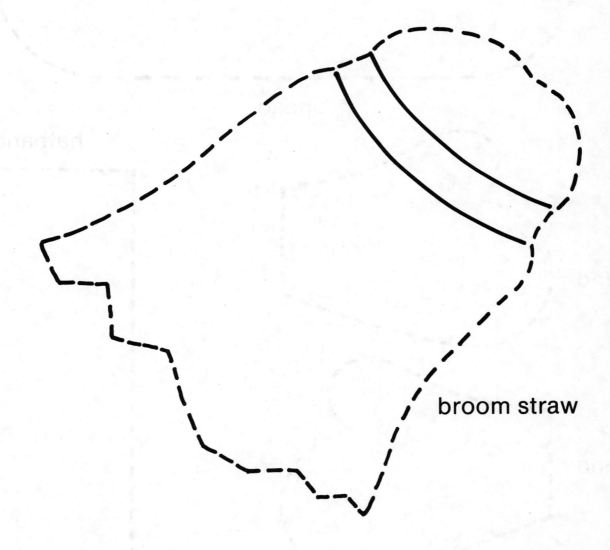

broom straw

Pattern C (yellow)

Witch 131

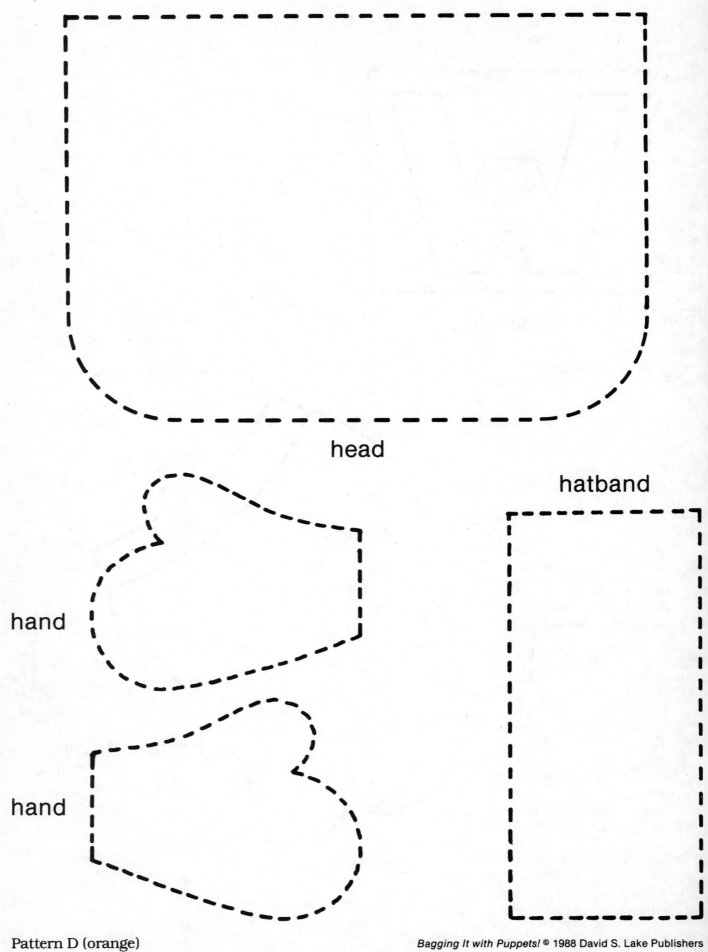

head

hatband

hand

hand

Pattern D (orange)

Bagging It with Puppets! © 1988 David S. Lake Publishers

132 Witch

X-Ray Boy

Materials: ☆

- paper lunch bags (11″ × 5¾″) for puppet base
- flesh tone construction paper (head, ears, hands)
- dark brown construction paper (hair)
- turquoise blue construction paper (arms)
- white construction paper (letter card, x–ray body)
- crayons
- scissors
- paper clips
- paper cutter
- patterns on pages 135–139

Preparation: ☆

1. Duplicate patterns on the appropriate colored construction paper.
2. For each child, make a packet containing:
   a) Pattern A (head, hands, ears)
   b) Pattern B (arms)
   c) Pattern C (hair)
   d) Pattern D (x–ray body)
   e) one letter card from Pattern E
   f) one paper lunch bag
   g) one paper clip
   Clip a–e together on the paper bag with the paper clip.

Procedure: ☆

1. Distribute to each student:
   a) paste
   b) crayons
   c) scissors
   d) puppet packet
   Demonstrate the following steps for the students.
2. Unclip the puppet packet and write your name on the back side of the paper lunch bag. Place the bag aside for now.
3. With black crayon, fill in the x-ray body, leaving the bones white. Color the letter *X* on the letter card black.
4. Cut all duplicated patterns along the dotted lines.
5. With one finger, put paste on the outside edge of the bag *(do not get paste on the flap)*. Place the x-ray body on the pasted edges and smooth down.

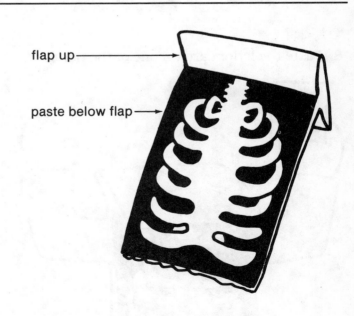

flap up —→

paste below flap —→

6. Run paste along the inside edge of each arm. Attach the arms below the flap in the creases of the bag.

7. Paste the hands behind the arms (thumbs facing in).

8. Paste the letter card on one of the hands.

9. Run paste along the top of the head. Place the hair on the head. Run paste along the straight edge of each ear. Paste them onto each side of the head.

10. With crayons, add the facial features. With white crayon, make two large ovals for the eyes. Outline the eyes with black; add pupils and lashes. Add the nose. With red crayon, add the mouth.

11. Apply paste to the outside edge of the flap.
12. Place the head on the pasted flap.
13. Let the puppet dry before using.

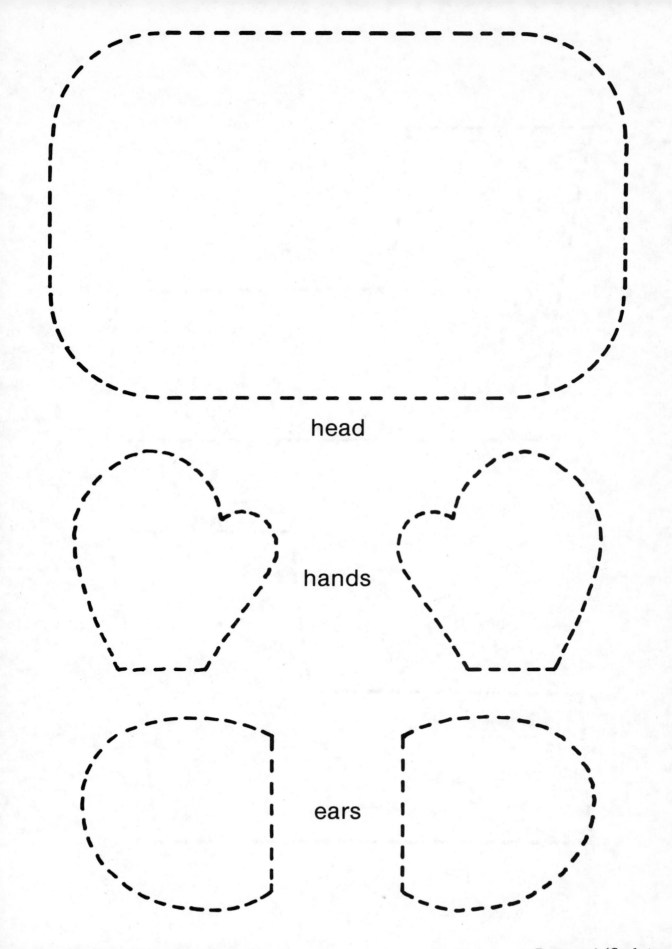

head

hands

ears

Pattern A (flesh tone)

X-Ray Boy   135

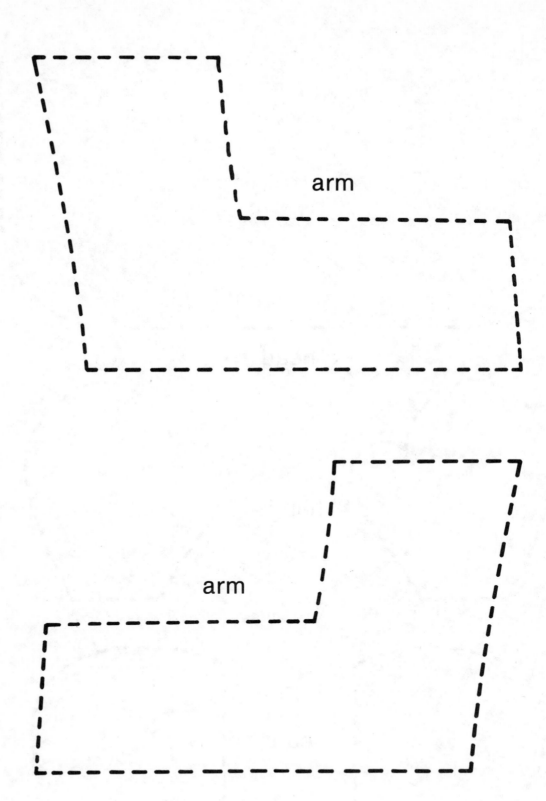

arm

arm

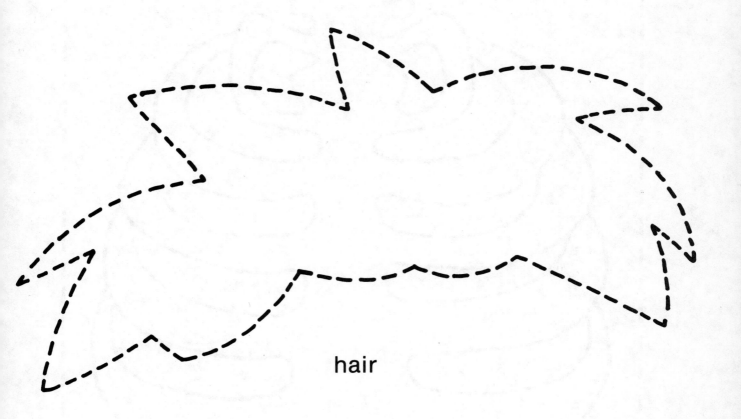

hair

Pattern C (dark brown)

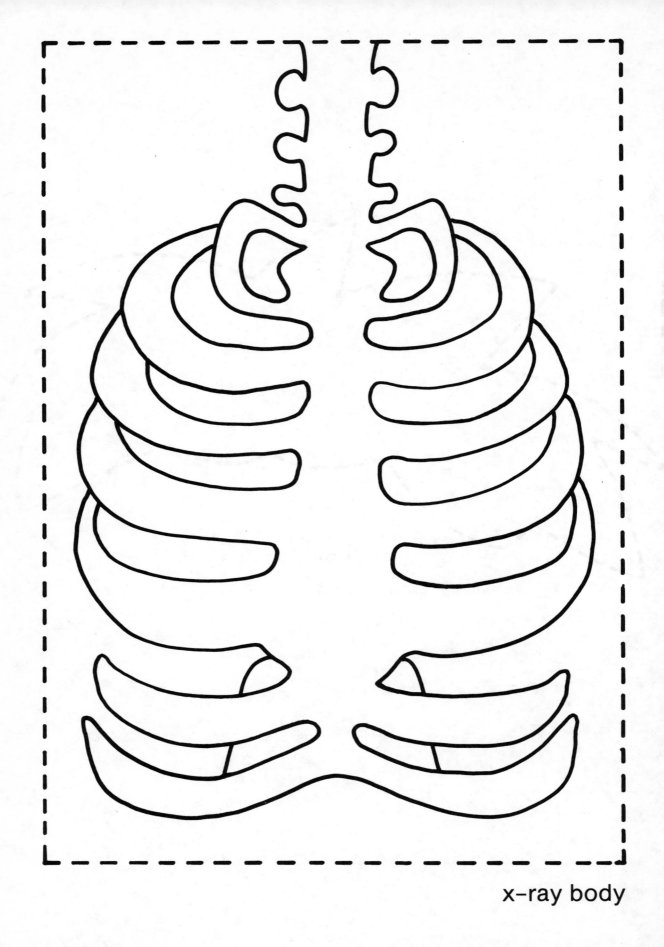

x-ray body

Pattern D (white)

Bagging It with Puppets! © 1988 David S. Lake Publishers

138   X-Ray Boy

letter card

letter card

letter card

letter card

Pattern E (white)

Yakky Yak

Materials:

- paper lunch bags (11″ × 5¾″) for puppet base
- orange construction paper (head, body)
- yellow construction paper (mane)
- red construction paper (mouth)
- white construction paper (horns, letter card)
- crayons
- scissors
- paste
- paper clips
- paper cutter
- patterns on pages 142–146

Preparation: ☆

1. Duplicate patterns on the appropriate colored construction paper.
2. For each child, make a packet containing:
   a) Pattern A (head)
   b) Pattern B (body)
   c) Pattern C (letter card, horns)
   d) Pattern D (mouth—upper and lower)
   e) Pattern E (mane)
   f) one paper lunch bag
   g) one paper clip
   Clip a–e together on the paper bag with the paper clip.

Procedure: ☆

1. Distribute to each student:
   a) paste
   b) crayons
   c) scissors
   d) puppet packet
   Demonstrate the following steps for the students.
2. Unclip the puppet packet and write your name on the back side of the paper lunch bag. Place the bag aside for now.
3. With black crayon, outline the head, the teeth, and the interior lines of the body. Color the letter *Y* on the letter card black.
4. Cut all duplicated patterns along the dotted lines.
5. With one finger, put paste on the outside edge of the bag (*do not get paste on the flap*). Place the body on the pasted edge and smooth down.

paste below flap

6. Paste the lower mouth below the fold of the flap.

fold

7. Paste the upper mouth on the *bottom side* of the flap.

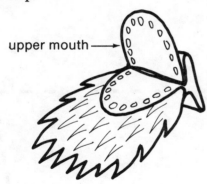

upper mouth →

8. Run paste along the top edge of the head. Place the mane on the head.

9. Apply paste to the inside edge of each horn. Paste the horns behind the mane.

10. With crayons, add the facial features. With the white crayon, draw two large ovals for the eyes. Outline the eyes with black; add lashes and pupils.

11. Apply paste to the outside edge of the flap. Place the head on the pasted flap and smooth down.

→ paste

12. Paste the letter card on the lower part of the body.
13. Let the puppet dry before using.

head

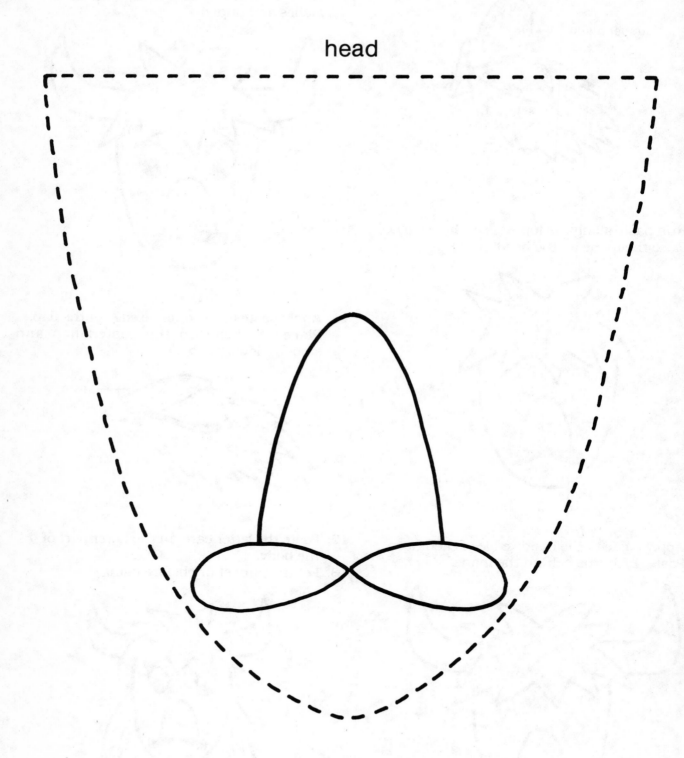

Pattern A (orange)

Bagging It with Puppets! © 1988 David S. Lake Publishers

body

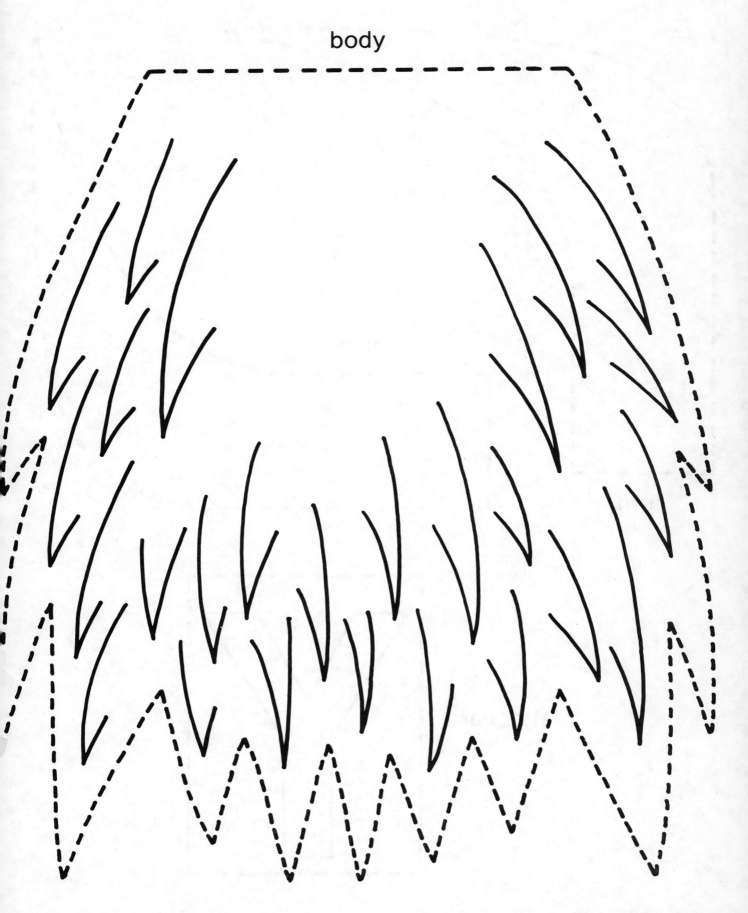

Pattern B (orange)

Yak 143

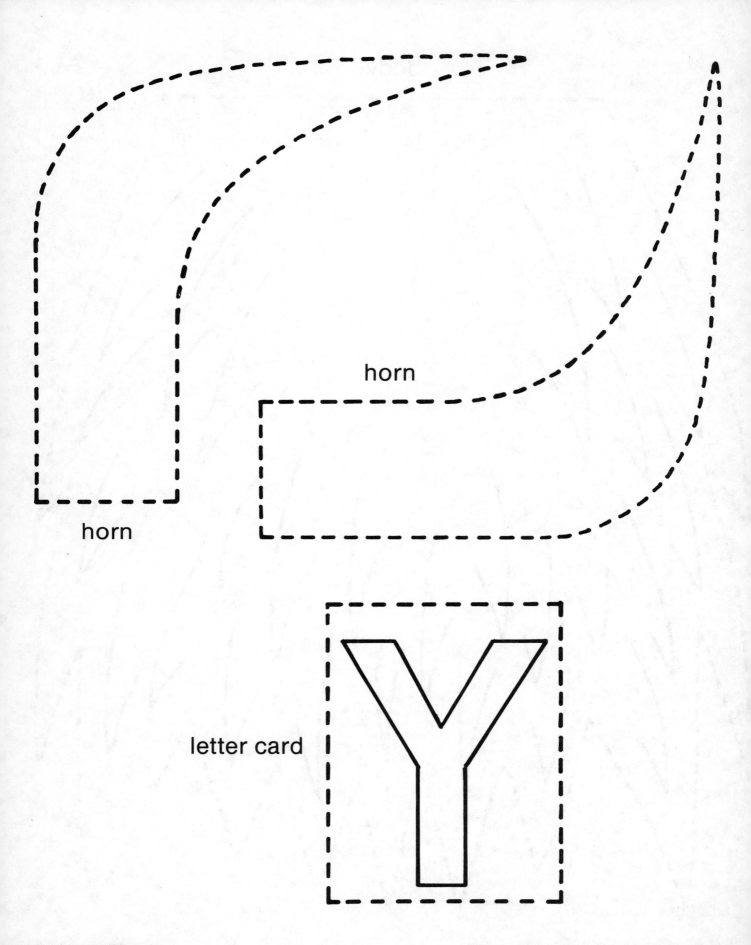

horn

horn

letter card

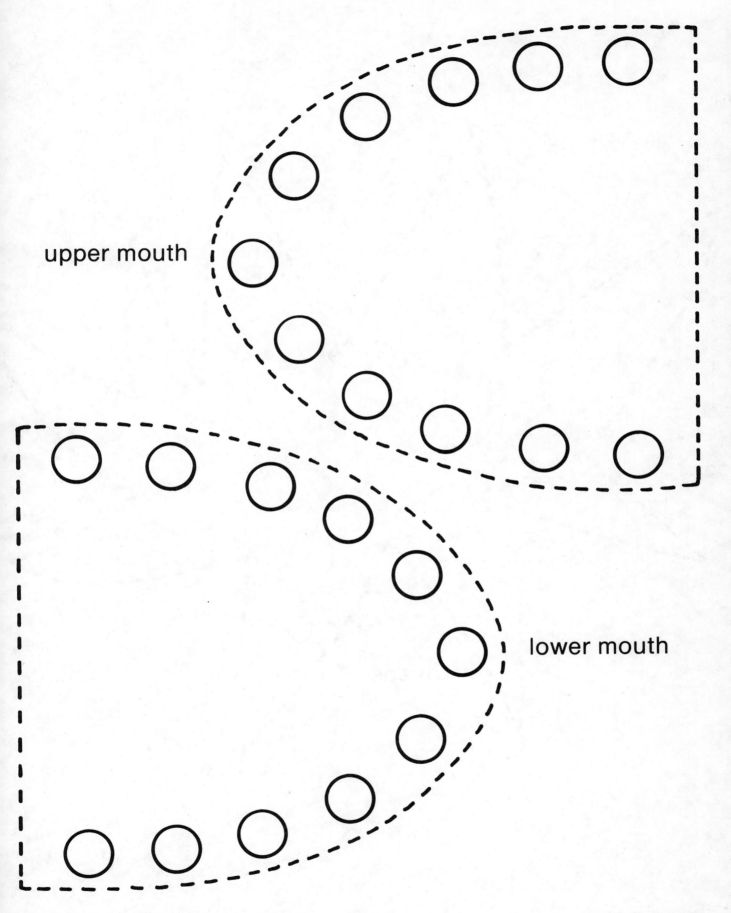

upper mouth

lower mouth

Pattern D (red)

Yak   145

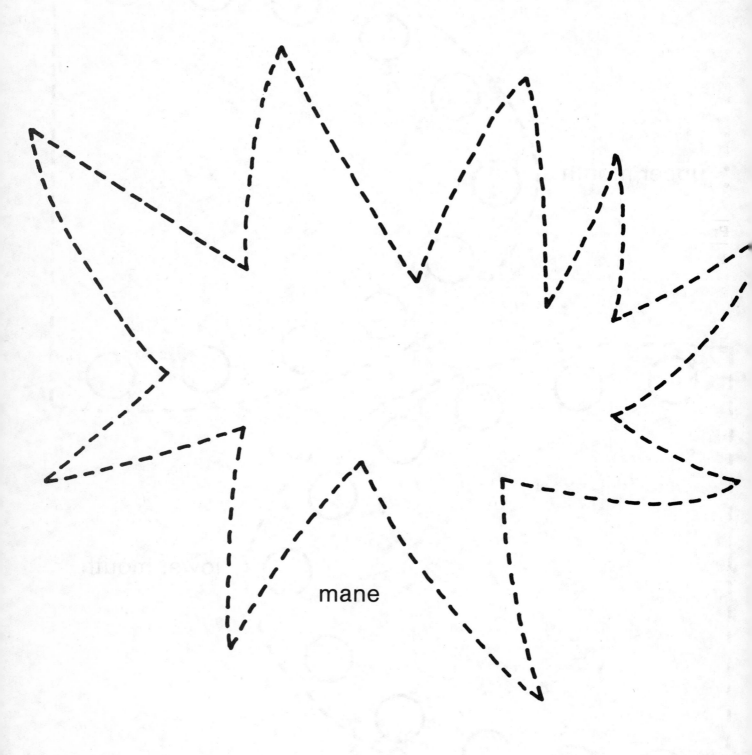

mane

Pattern E (yellow)

Zeke Zebra

Materials: ☆

- paper lunch bags (11″ × 5¾″) for puppet base
- black construction paper (mane)
- white construction paper (body, head, letter card)
- red construction paper (mouth)
- crayons
- scissors
- paste
- paper clips
- paper cutter
- patterns on pages 149–153

Preparation: ☆

1. Duplicate patterns on the appropriate colored construction paper.
2. Using a paper cutter, cut sheets of construction paper 11″ × 4″ for the mane. You can cut four to five sheets at a time.
3. For each child, make a packet containing:
   a) Pattern A (head)
   b) Pattern B (upper mouth)
   c) Pattern C (lower mouth)
   d) Pattern D (body)
   e) one letter card from Pattern E
   f) one precut rectangle for the mane
   g) one paper lunch bag
   h) one paper clip
   Clip a–f together on the paper bag with the paper clip.

Procedure: ☆

1. Distribute to each student:
   a) paste
   b) crayons
   c) scissors
   d) puppet packet
   Demonstrate the following steps for the students.
2. Unclip the puppet packet and write your name on the back side of the paper lunch bag. Place the bag aside for now.
3. With black crayon, color in the stripes on the head and body.
4. With white crayon, color in the teeth.
5. With red crayon, color in the letter Z on the letter card.
6. With pink crayon, color in the nostrils and the inner part of the ears.
7. With black crayon, color in the pupils and the mane between the ears. Outline the lashes, the eyes, and the nostrils.
8. Cut all duplicated patterns along the dotted lines.
9. With one finger, put paste on the outside edge of the bag (*do not get paste on the flap*). Place the body on the pasted edge and smooth down.

— paste below flap

10. With one finger, put paste below the fold of the flap. Paste the lower mouth below the fold.

fold of bag

11. Apply paste to the outside edge of the flap.

12. Place the head on the pasted flap and smooth down.

13. Apply paste to the inside edge of the head. Paste the upper mouth down.

fold of bag

14. Fold the edge of the black 11″ × 4″ rectangle as shown.

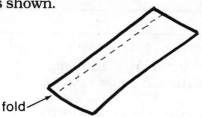

fold

15. To form the mane, make horizontal cuts to the folded edge.

16. Paste the mane on the back of the bag.

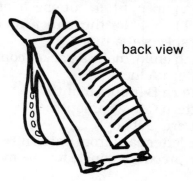

back view

17. Paste the letter card to the lower body.

18. Let the puppet dry before using.

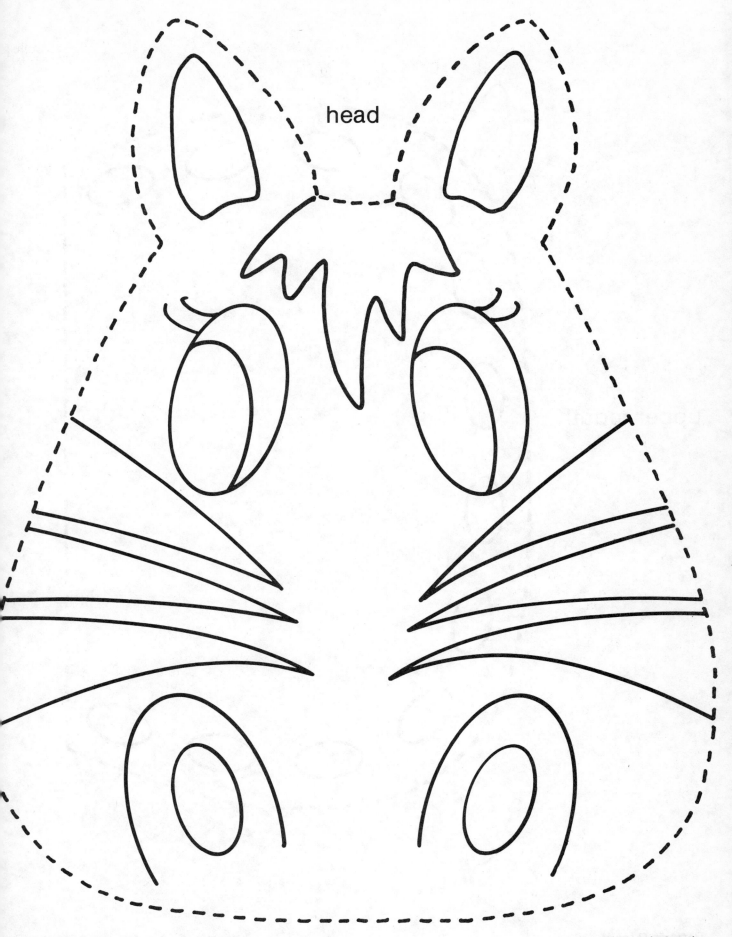

head

Pattern A (white)

Zebra   149

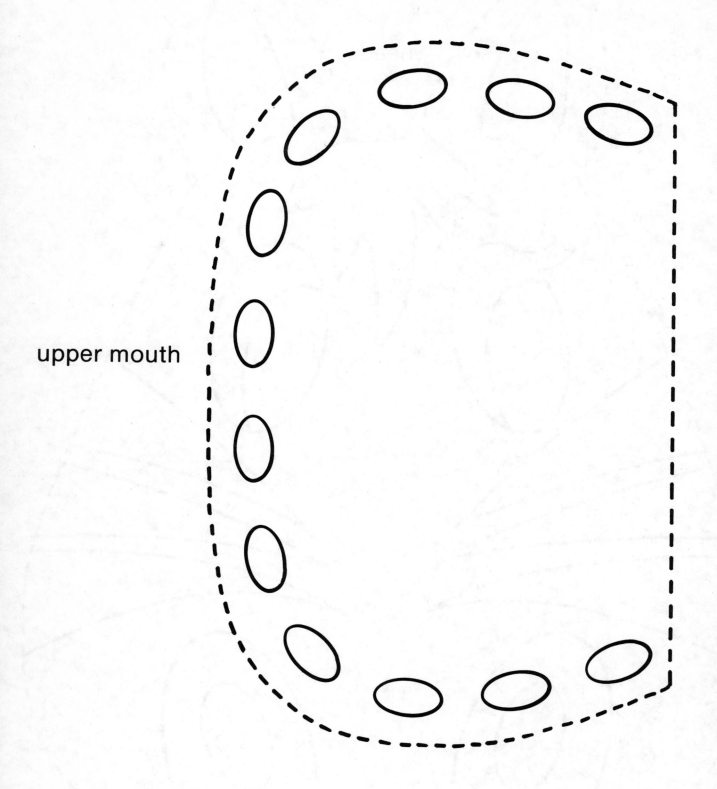

upper mouth

Bagging It with Puppets! © 1988 David S. Lake Publishers

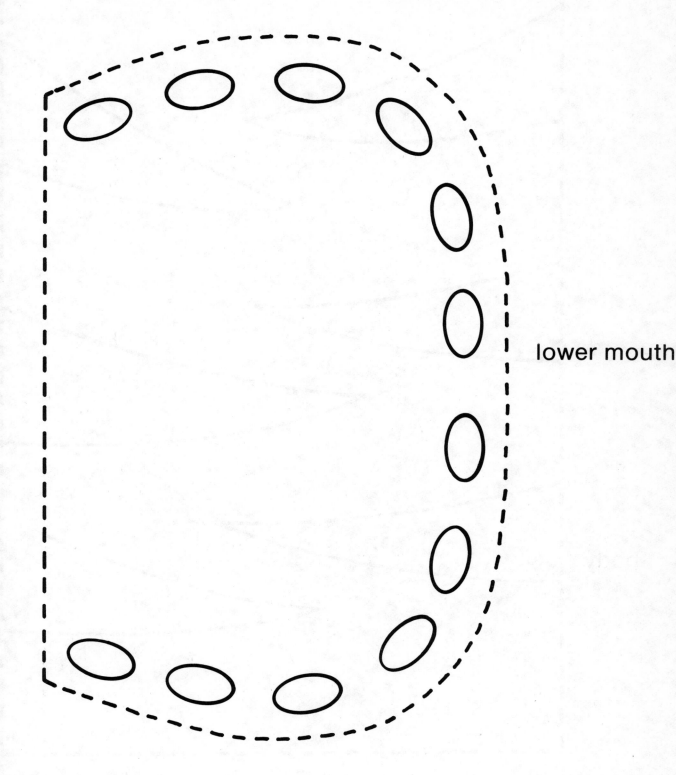

lower mouth

Pattern C (red)

Zebra   151

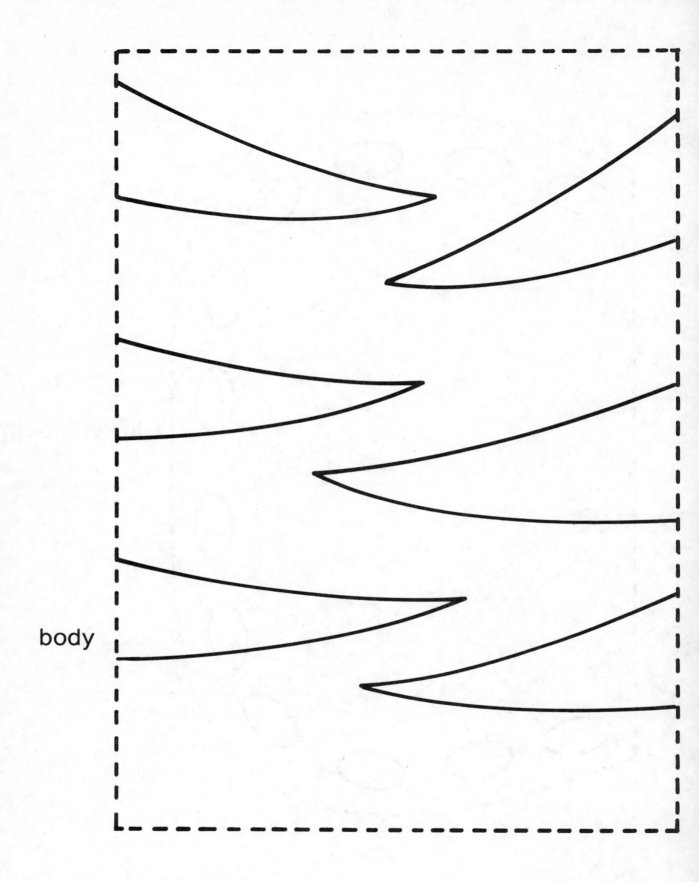

body

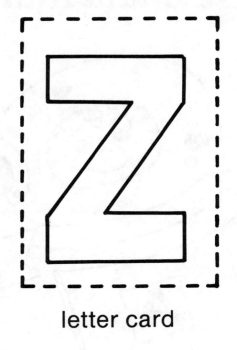

letter card

letter card

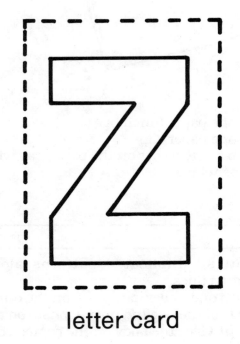

letter card

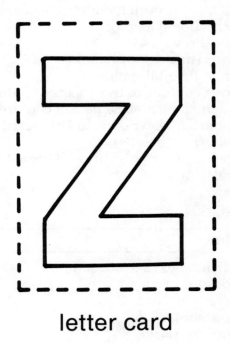

letter card

Pattern E (white)

Astronaut Andy or Astronaut Annie

Materials: ☆

- paper lunch bags (11″ × 5¾″) for puppet base
- yellow construction paper (gloves, letter card, collar)
- turquoise blue construction paper (body, arms, helmet)
- brown construction paper (face)
- crayons
- scissors
- paste
- paper clips
- paper cutter
- patterns on pages 156–157

Preparation: ☆

1. Duplicate patterns on the appropriate colored construction paper. *(This puppet can be either male or female.)*
2. Using a paper cutter, cut sheets of orange construction paper for:
   a) face (brown), 4½″ × 5″
   b) arms (turquoise blue), 2″ × 5″
   c) body (turquoise blue), 6″ × 9″
   You can cut four to five sheets at a time.
3. For each child, make a packet containing:
   a) Pattern A (gloves, collar, letter card)
   b) Pattern B (helmet)
   c) one face (4½″ × 5″ brown sheet)
   d) one body
   e) two arms
   f) one paper lunch bag
   g) one paper clip
   Clip a–e together on the paper bag with the paper clip.

Procedure: ☆

1. Distribute to each student:
   a) paste
   b) crayons
   c) scissors
   d) puppet packet
   Demonstrate the following steps for the students.
2. Unclip the puppet packet and write your name on the back side of the paper lunch bag. Place the bag aside for now.
3. With black crayon, outline the interior lines of the puppet. Color in the letter *A* and the circles on the helmet with black crayon.

4. Cut all duplicated patterns along the dotted lines.
5. With one finger, put paste on the outside edge of the bag *(do not get paste on the flap)*. Place the body on the pasted edge and smooth down.

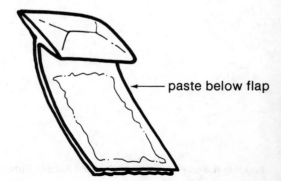

paste below flap

6. Run paste along the inside edge of each arm. Attach the arms below the flap, in the creases of the bag.

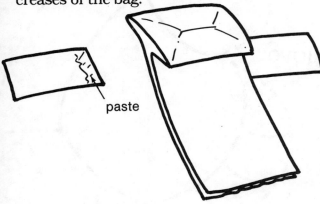

paste

7. Paste the letter card on the bottom of the body.
8. Paste the gloves, thumbs up, onto the arms.

9. Run paste along the border of the inside circle on the back side of the helmet. Place the brown face sheet on the paste.
10. Run paste along the top edge of the collar. Place the helmet over the collar.

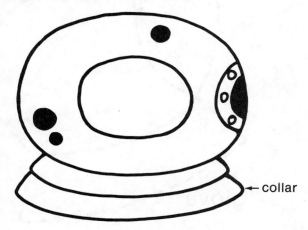

← collar

11. With crayons, add facial features to the face. With white crayon, color two large ovals for the eyes. Outline the eyes with black, and add pupils and lashes. Add the nose. With red crayon, add the mouth. Then add the hair.

12. Apply paste to the outside edge of the flap.

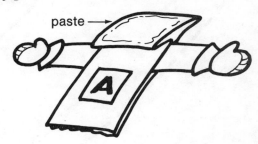

paste →

13. Place the head on the pasted flap.
14. Let the puppet dry before using.

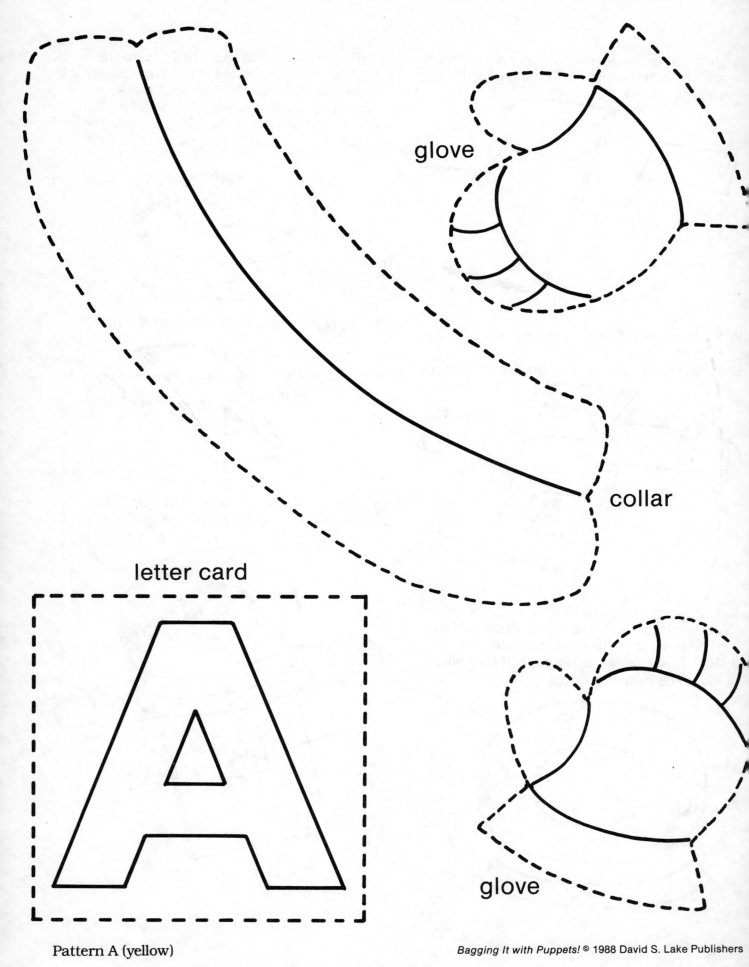

glove

collar

letter card

A

glove

Pattern A (yellow)

Bagging It with Puppets! © 1988 David S. Lake Publishers

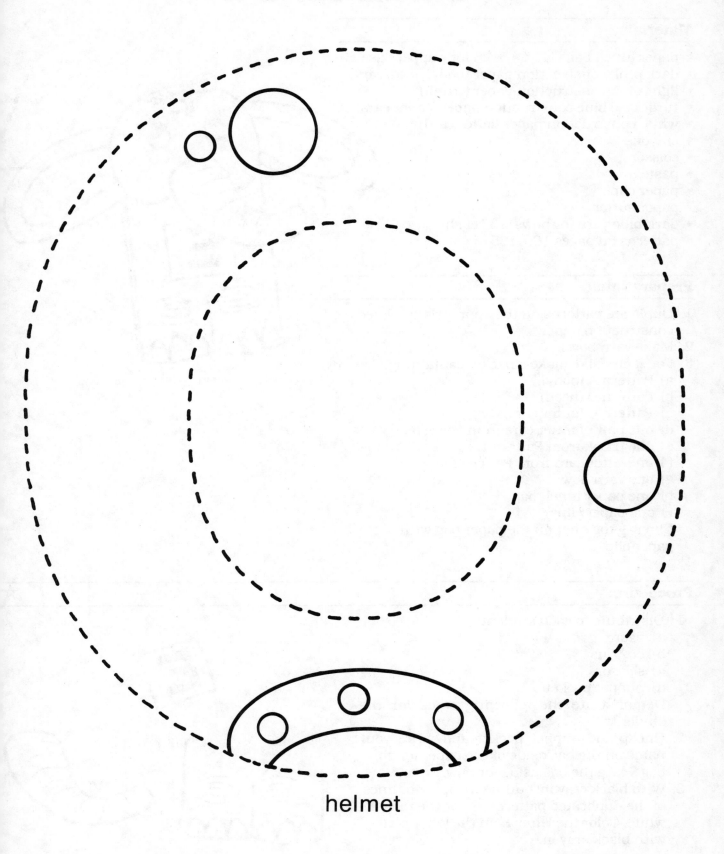

helmet

Pattern B (turquoise blue)

Ellie Elephant

Materials: ☆

- paper lunch bags (11″ × 5¾″) for puppet base
- dark pink construction paper (body, head, ears)
- light pink construction paper (trunk)
- turquoise blue construction paper (inner ears)
- white construction paper (letter card)
- crayons
- scissors
- paste
- paper clips
- paper cutter
- dark blue yarn for bows, 13″ each
- patterns on pages 160–165

Preparation: ☆

1. Duplicate patterns on the appropriate colored construction paper.
2. Make yarn bows.
3. For each child, make a packet containing:
   a) Pattern A (body)
   b) Pattern B (head)
   c) Pattern C (outer ears)
   d) one pair of inner ears from Pattern D
   e) one trunk from Pattern E
   f) one letter card from Pattern F
   g) one yarn bow
   h) one paper lunch bag
   i) one paper clip
   Clip a–g together on the paper bag with the paper clip.

Procedure: ☆

1. Distribute to each student:
   a) paste
   b) crayons
   c) scissors
   d) puppet packet
   Demonstrate the following steps for the students.
2. Unclip the puppet packet and write your name on the back side of the paper lunch bag. Place the bag aside for now.
3. With black crayon, outline the interior lines of the duplicated patterns. Color the toenails white. Color the letter *E* on the letter card with black crayon.

4. Cut all duplicated patterns along the dotted lines.

5. With one finger, put paste on the outside edge of the bag (*do not get paste on the flap*). Place the body on the pasted edge and smooth down.

paste below flap →

6. Paste the letter card on the lower body, above the knees.

7. Paste the blue inner ears on the large pink outer ears. Paste the ears behind the head. Paste on the trunk.

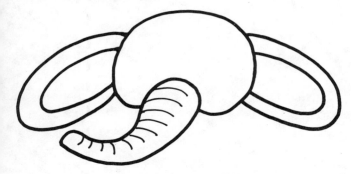

8. With white crayon, color two large ovals for the eyes. Outline the eyes with black crayon and add black pupils and lashes.

9. Apply paste to the outside edge of the flap.

flap →

10. Place the head on the pasted flap.
11. Paste the yarn bow on the head.
12. Let the puppet dry before using.

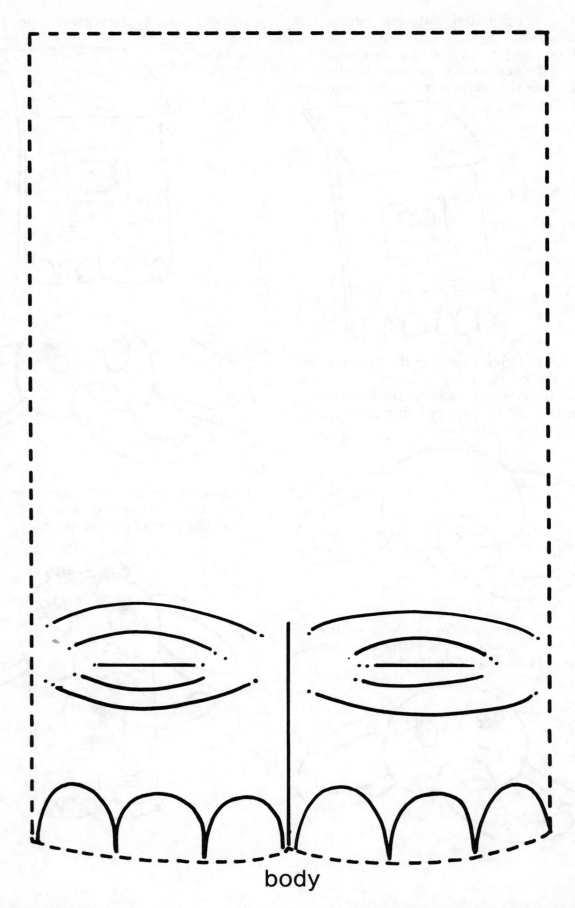

body

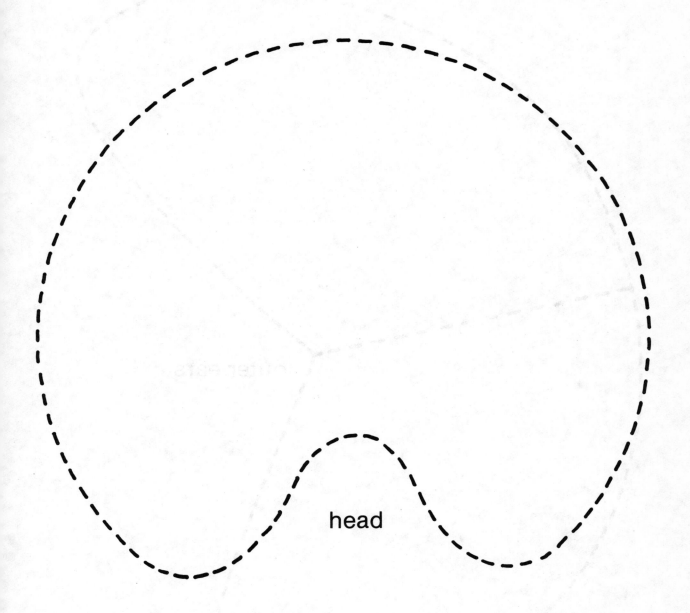

head

Pattern B (dark pink)

Ellie   161

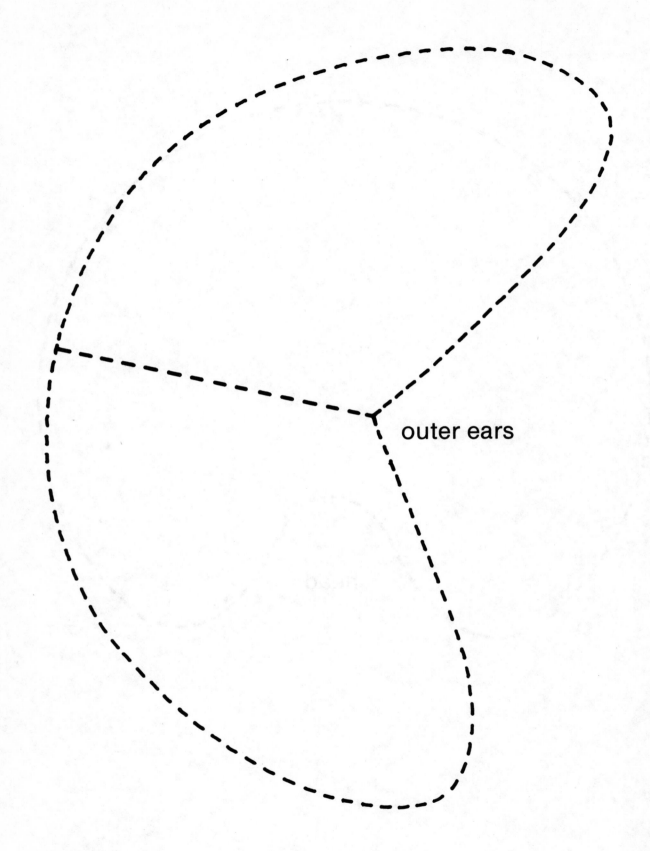

outer ears

Pattern C (dark pink)

Bagging It with Puppets! © 1988 David S. Lake Publisher

162   Ellie

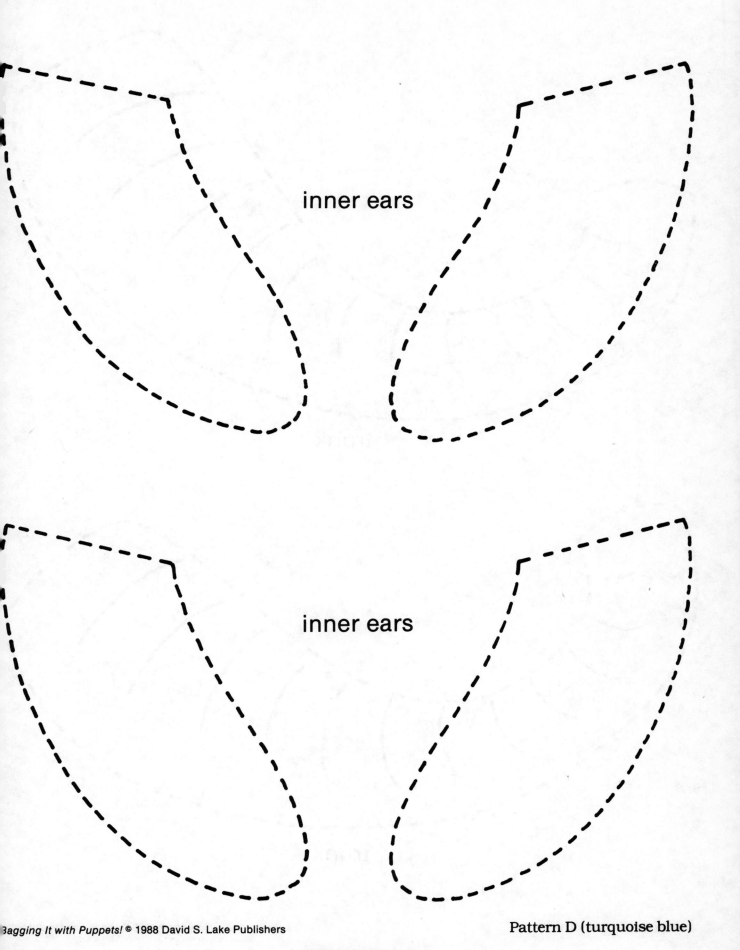

inner ears

inner ears

Pattern D (turquoise blue)

Ellie 163

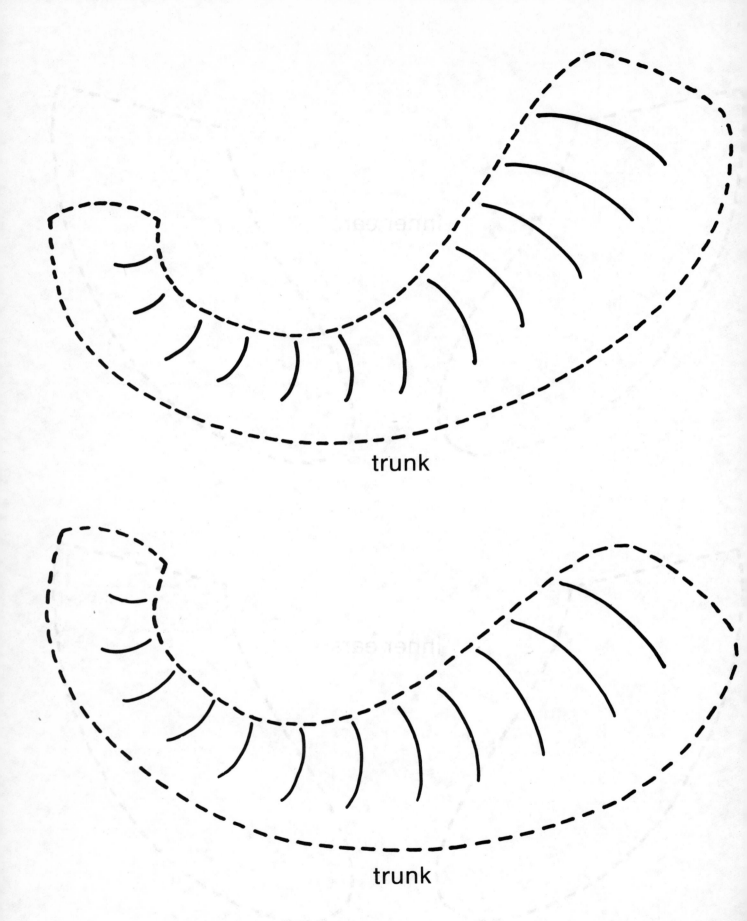

trunk

trunk

Pattern E (light pink)

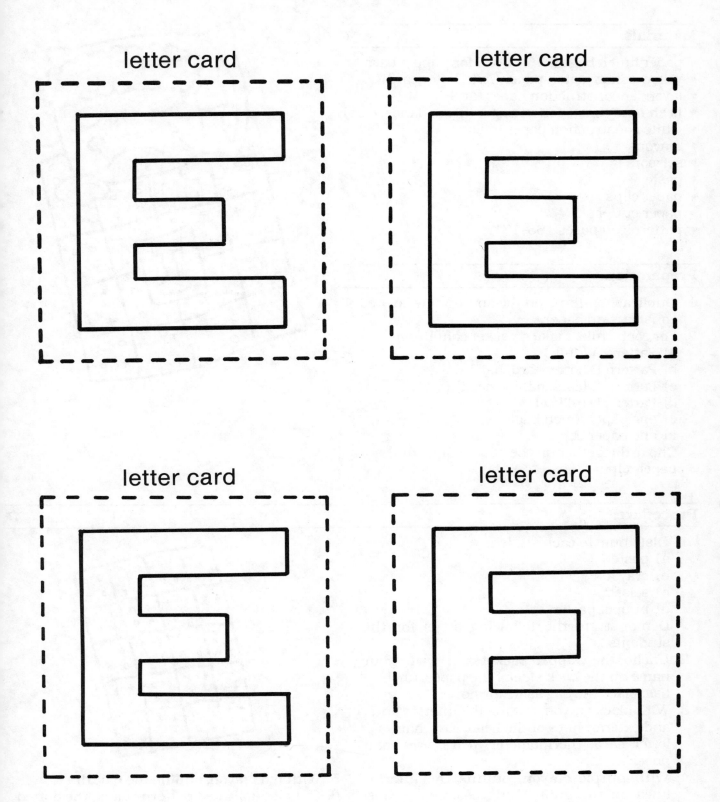

letter card

letter card

letter card

letter card

Pattern F (white)

Ill Izzy

Materials: ☆

- paper lunch bags (11″ × 5¾″) for puppet base
- yellow construction paper (hair, letter card)
- lavender construction paper (quilt)
- flesh tone construction paper (head, hands, ears)
- white construction paper (pillow)
- crayons
- scissors
- paste
- paper clips
- paper cutter
- patterns on pages 168–171

Preparation: ☆

1. Duplicate patterns on the appropriate colored construction paper.
2. For each child, make a packet containing:
   a) Pattern A (quilt)
   b) Pattern B (letter card, hair)
   c) Pattern C (ears, hands, head)
   d) Pattern D (pillow)
   e) one paper lunch bag
   f) one paper clip
   Clip a–d together on the paper bag with the paper clip.

Procedure: ☆

1. Distribute to each student:
   a) paste
   b) crayons
   c) scissors
   d) puppet packet
   Demonstrate the following steps for the students.
2. Unclip the puppet packet and write your name on the back side of the paper lunch bag. Place the bag aside for now.
3. With black crayon, outline the interior lines and exterior lines of the head, ears, hair, letter card, thermometer, tears, eyes, and nose.
4. With purple crayon, outline the interior lines on the quilt. Using colored crayons, add texture to each quilt block.

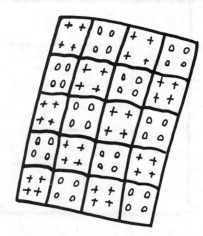

5. With red crayon, outline the mouth.
6. Cut all duplicated patterns along the dotted lines.

7. With one finger, put paste on the outside edge of the bag *(do not get paste on the flap)*. Place the quilt on the pasted edge and smooth down.

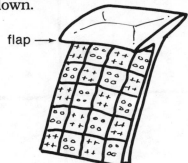

flap →

8. Run paste along the straight edge of the head. Paste on the hair.

paste

9. Apply paste to the straight edge of the ears and attach them below the hair, on the back side of the head.

paste

10. Put a dot of paste at the lower edge of the face *(right and left)*. Paste on the hands.

11. Apply paste to the outside edge of the paper bag's flap. Place the pillow on the pasted flap and smooth down.

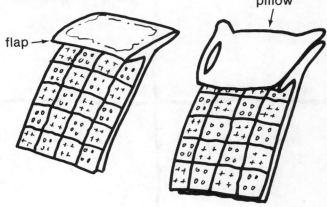

pillow

flap →

12. Apply paste to the outside edge of the head on the back side.

paste →

13. Place the head on the pillow and smooth down.
14. Paste the letter card on the quilt.
15. Let the puppet dry before using.

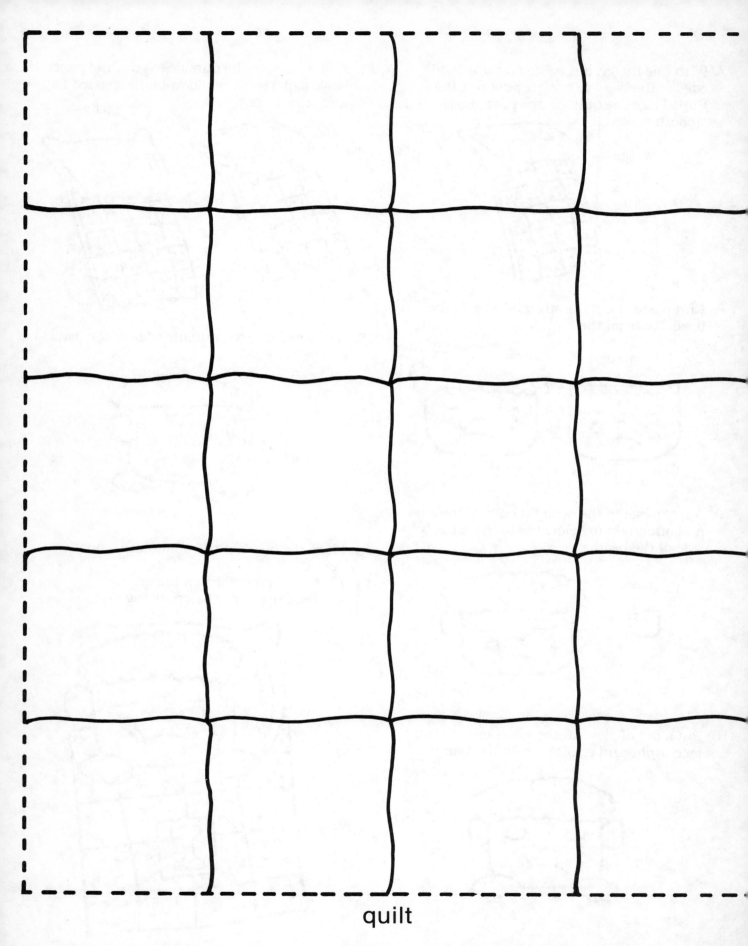

quilt

Pattern A (lavender)

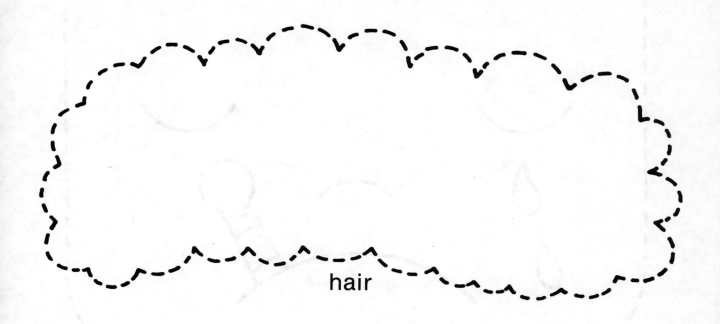

hair

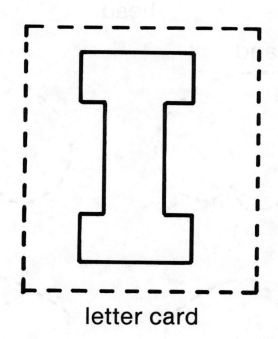

letter card

Pattern B (yellow)

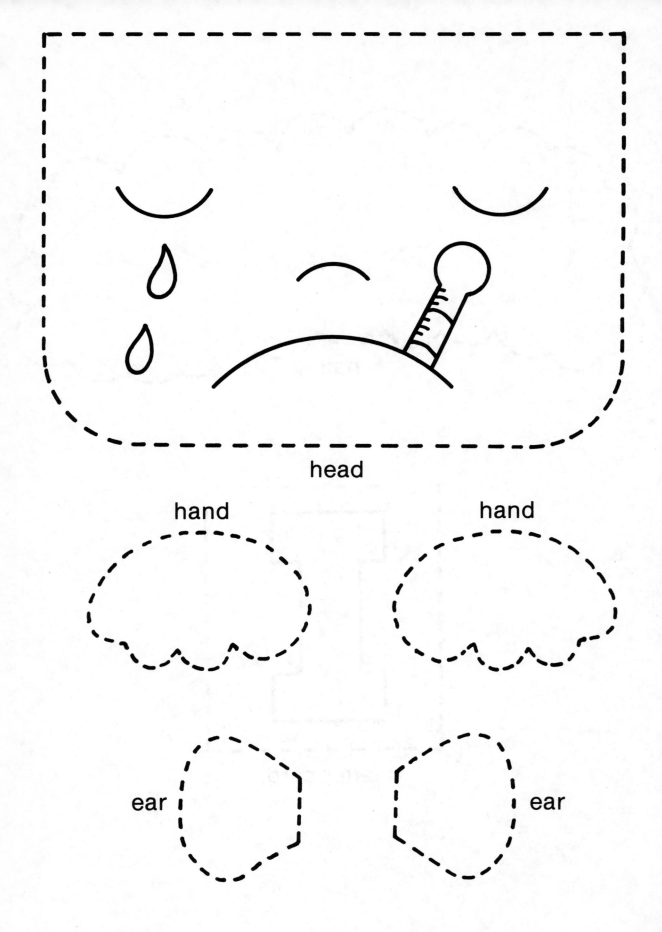

head

hand   hand

ear   ear

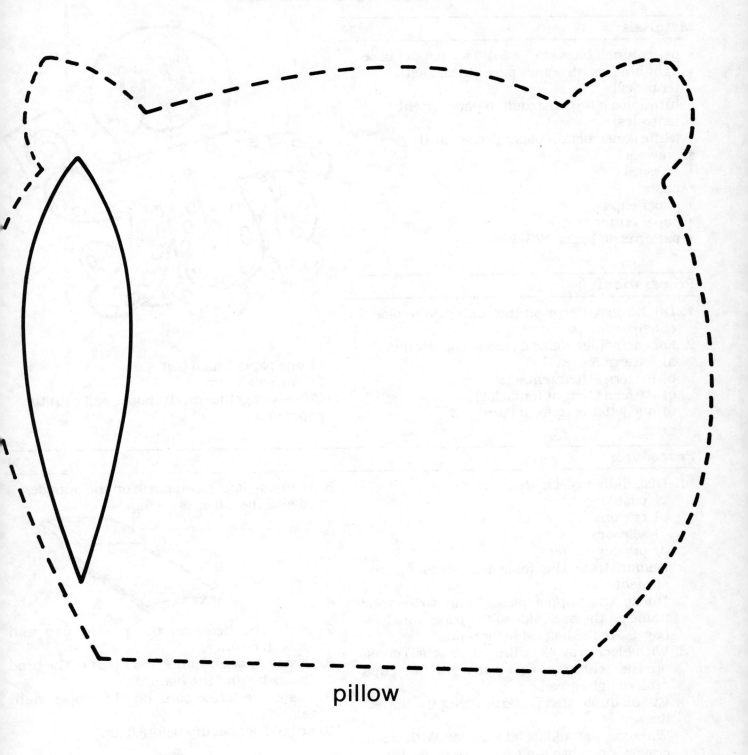

pillow

Pattern D (white)

Ollie Octopus

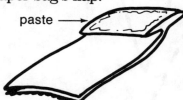

Materials: ☆

- paper lunch bags (11″ × 5¾″) for puppet base
- light blue construction paper (head, left tentacles)
- turquoise blue construction paper (right tentacles)
- white construction paper (letter card)
- crayons
- scissors
- paste
- paper clips
- paper cutter
- patterns on pages 173–176

Preparation: ☆

1. Duplicate patterns on the appropriate colored construction paper.
2. For each child, make a packet containing:
   a) Pattern A (head)
   b) Pattern B (left tentacles)
   c) Pattern C (right tentacles)
   d) one letter card from Pattern D
   e) one paper lunch bag
   f) one paper clip
   Clip a–d together on the paper bag with the paper clip.

Procedure: ☆

1. Distribute to each student:
   a) paste
   b) crayons
   c) scissors
   d) puppet packet
   Demonstrate the following steps for the students.
2. Unclip the puppet packet and write your name on the back side of the paper lunch bag. Place the bag aside for now.
3. With black crayon, outline the suction cups on the tentacles. Color the suction cups pink or light green.
4. Cut all duplicated patterns along the dotted lines.
5. With crayons, add facial features. With white crayon, draw two large white ovals for the eyes. Outline them with black and add pupils and lashes. With red crayon, add the mouth.

6. With one finger, put paste on the outside edge of the paper bag's flap.

paste →

7. Place the head on the pasted flap and smooth down.
8. Paste tentacles on the lower part of the head (*paste behind the head*).
9. Paste the letter card on the upper right tentacle.
10. Let the puppet dry before using.

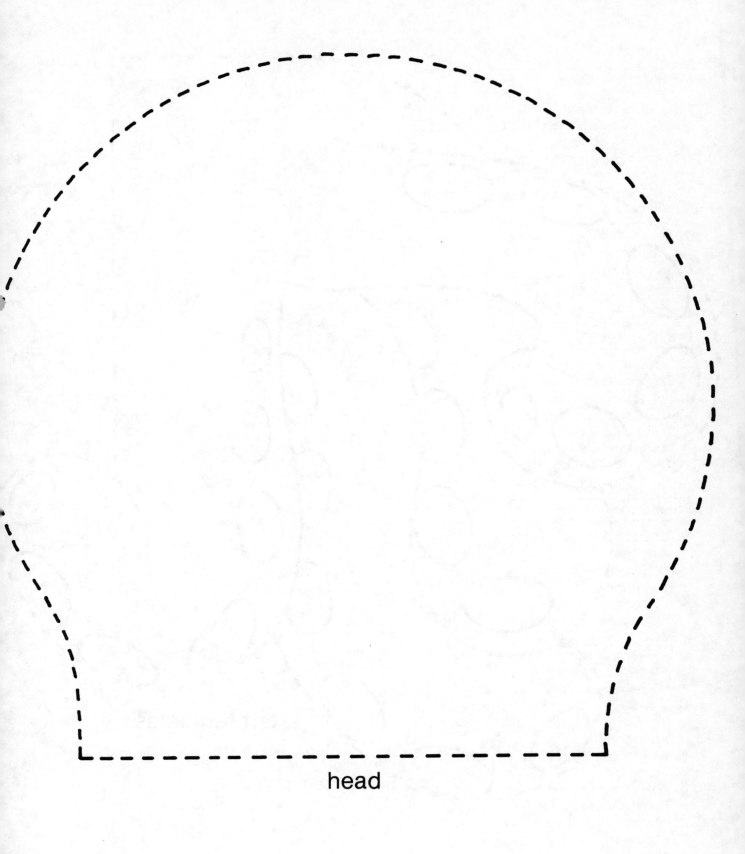

head

Pattern A (light blue)

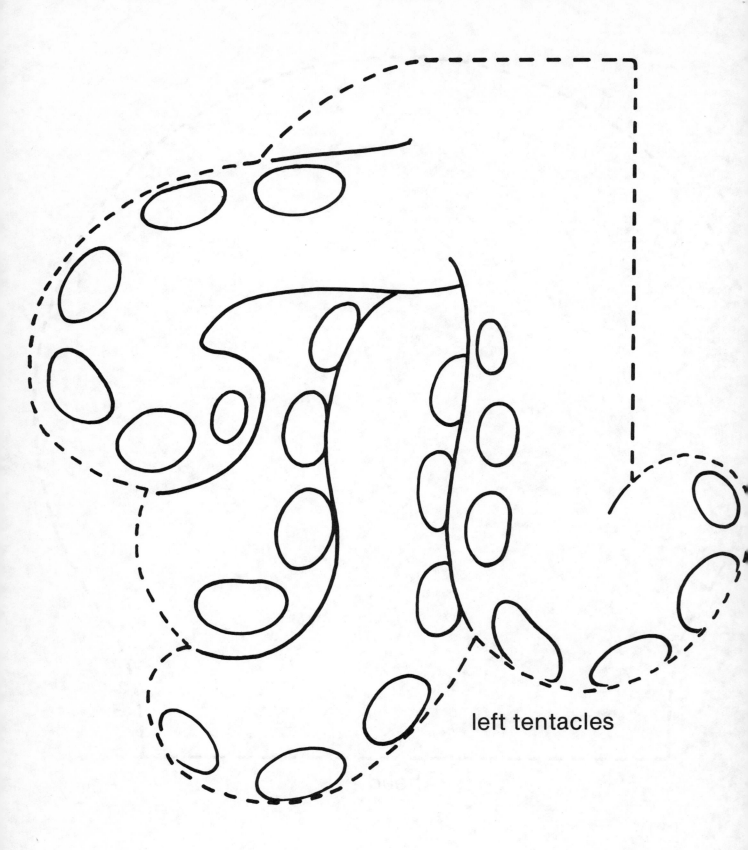

left tentacles

Bagging It with Puppets! © 1988 David S. Lake Publishers

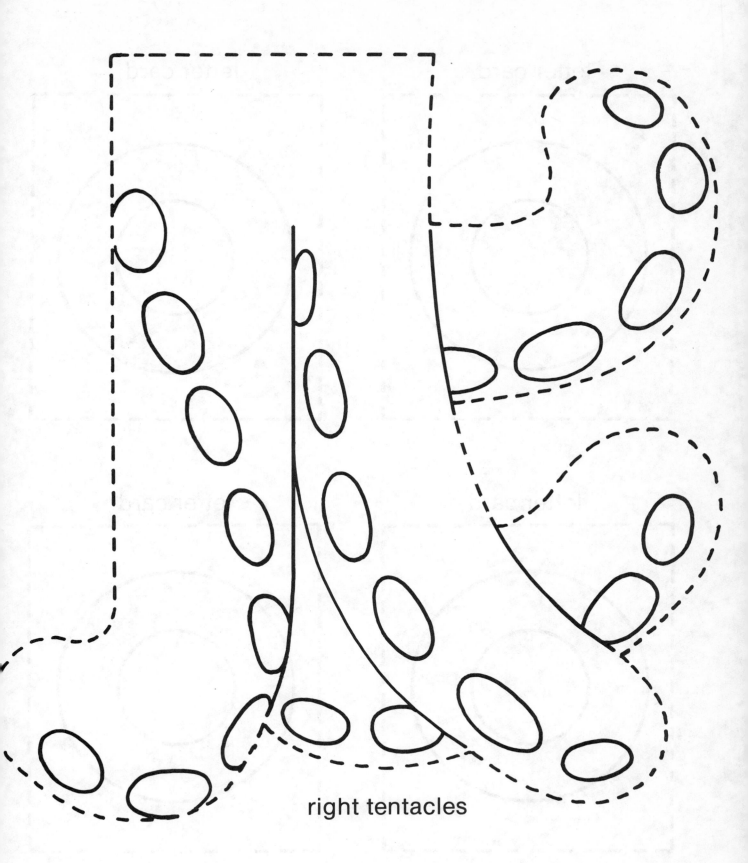

right tentacles

Pattern C (turquoise blue)

letter card   letter card

letter card   letter card

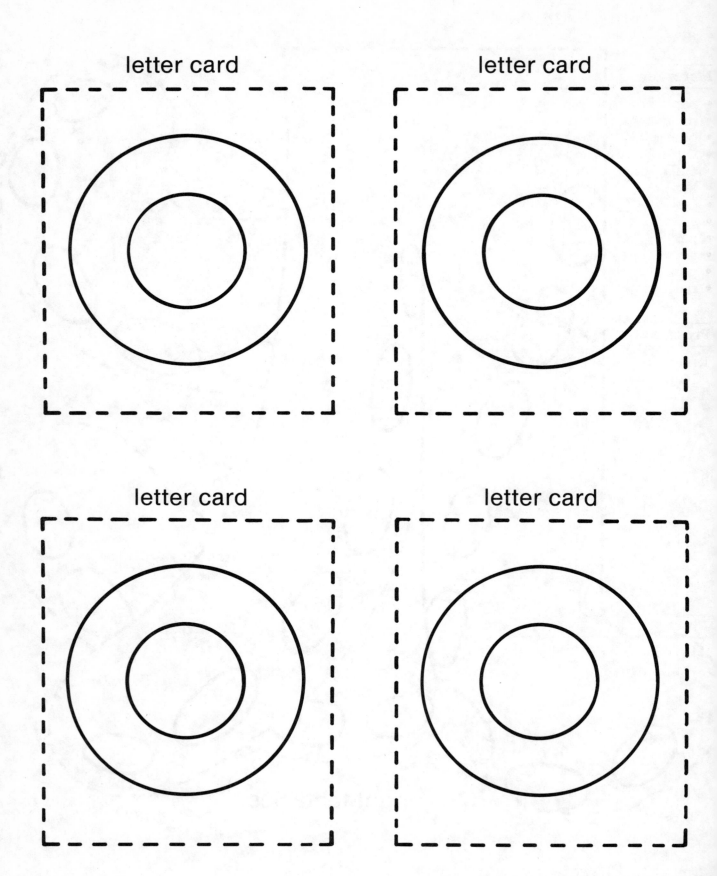

Pattern D (white)

Bagging It with Puppets! © 1988 David S. Lake Publishers

176 Ollie

Uncle Sam

Materials: ☆

- paper lunch bags (11″ × 5¾″) for puppet base
- red construction paper (hat)
- blue construction paper (sleeves, jacket)
- white construction paper (hair, stripes, beard, cuffs, letter card)
- flesh tone construction paper (face, hands)
- crayons
- scissors
- paste
- paper clips
- paper cutter
- patterns on pages 179–182

Preparation: ☆

1. Duplicate patterns on the appropriate colored construction paper.
2. Using a paper cutter, cut sheets of construction paper for:
   a) arms (blue), 2″ × 4″
   b) jacket (blue), 6″ × 9″
   You can cut four to five sheets at a time.
3. For each child, make a packet containing:
   a) Pattern A (hat)
   b) Pattern B (hair, beard)
   c) Pattern C (cuffs, hat stripes, letter card)
   d) Pattern D (face, hands)
   e) two precut arms
   f) one precut jacket

   g) one paper lunch bag
   h) one paper clip
   Clip a–f together on the paper bag with the paper clip.

Procedure: ☆

1. Distribute to each student:
   a) paste
   b) crayons
   c) scissors
   d) puppet packet
   Demonstrate the following steps for the students.
2. Unclip the puppet packet and write your name on the back side of the paper lunch bag. Place the bag aside for now.
3. With black crayon, outline the hatband.
4. With blue crayon, color the stars in the hatband.
5. Color the letter *U* on the letter card red.

6. Cut all duplicated patterns along the dotted lines.
7. With one finger, put paste on the outside edge of the bag (*do not get paste on the flap*). Place the jacket on the pasted edge and smooth down.

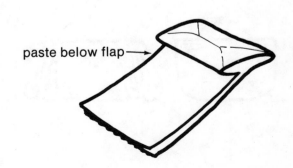

paste below flap →

8. Run paste along the inside edge of each sleeve. Attach the sleeves below the flap, in the creases of the bag.

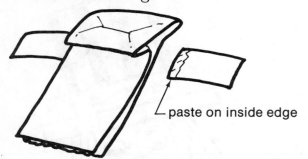

paste on inside edge

9. Paste white cuffs on the outside edges of the sleeves.

← cuff

10. Turn the puppet over and apply paste to the inside edge of each hand. Paste the hands, thumbs up, behind the sleeves.

11. Run paste along the straight edge of the head. Attach the hair. Cut the hair along the dotted lines and curl the ends with a pencil.

paste   hair

12. Run paste along the straight edge of the head again. Place the hat on the pasted edge.

13. Paste vertical white stripes on the hat.

14. With crayons, add the facial features. With white crayon, draw two large ovals for eyes. Outline the eyes with black. Add pupils and lashes. Add the nose. With red crayon, add the mouth. Paste on the beard.

15. Paste the letter card to the jacket.
16. Let the puppet dry before using.

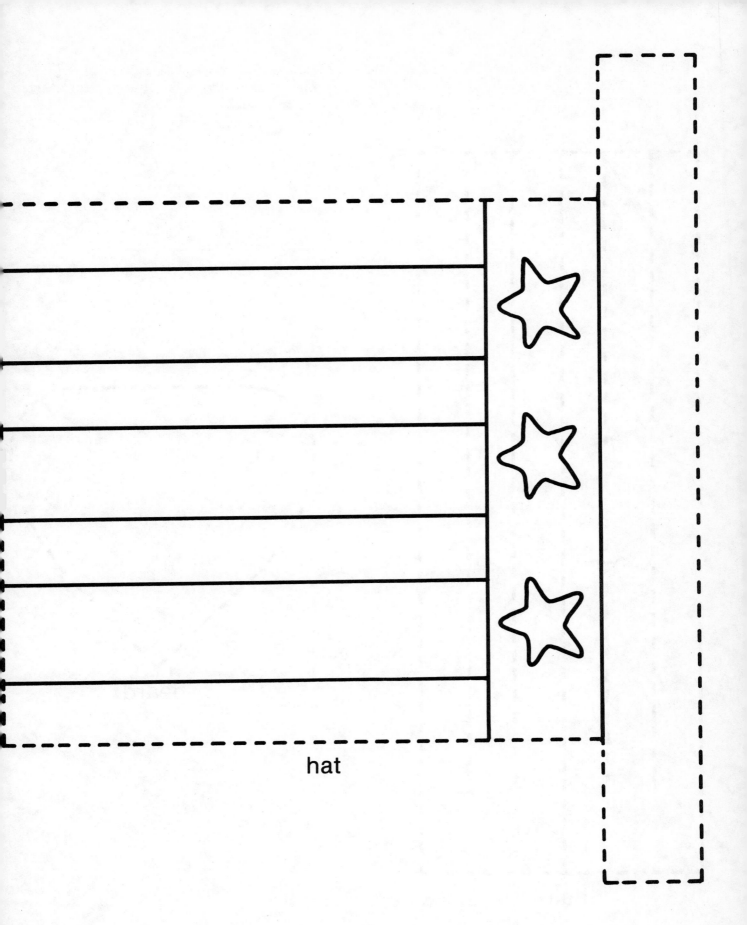

hat

Pattern A (red)

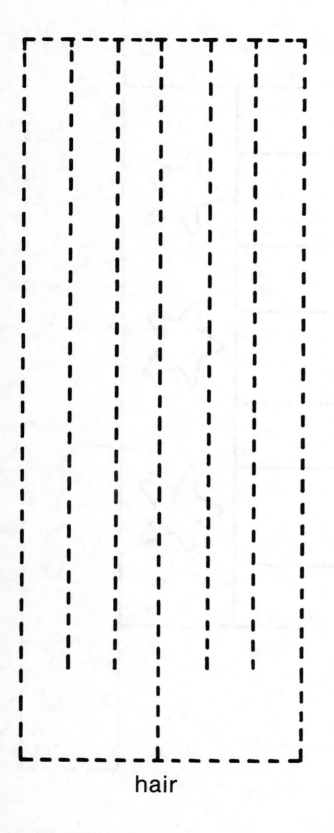

hair

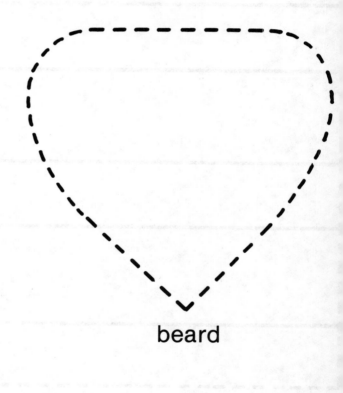

beard

Pattern B (white)

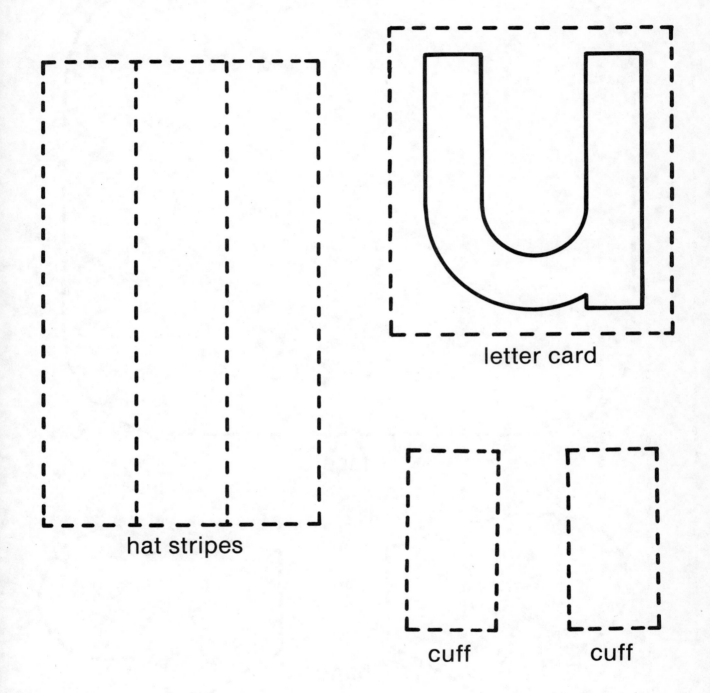

hat stripes

letter card

cuff   cuff

Pattern C (white)

Uncle Sam 181

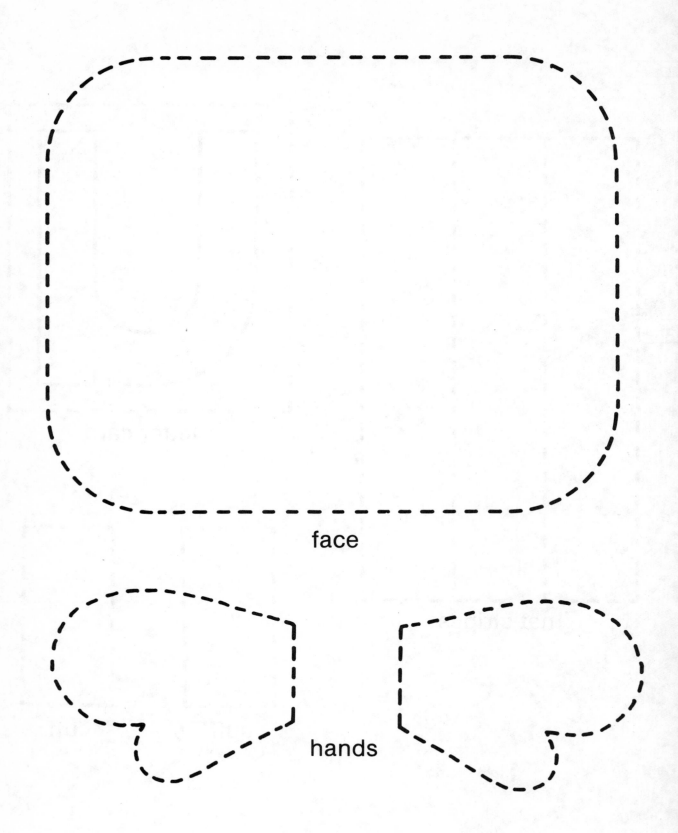

face

hands

Pattern D (flesh tone)

Bagging It with Puppets! © 1988 David S. Lake Publishers

Amy Angel

Materials: ☆

- paper lunch bags (11″ × 5¾″) for puppet base
- yellow construction paper (wings, letter card)
- pink construction paper (body)
- white construction paper (halo)
- flesh tone construction paper (face)
- brown construction paper (hair)
- crayons
- scissors
- paste
- paper clips
- paper cutter
- patterns on pages 185–189

Preparation: ☆

1. Duplicate patterns on the appropriate colored construction paper.
2. For each child, make a packet containing:
   a) Pattern A (wings, letter card)
   b) Pattern B (body)
   c) one halo from Pattern C
   d) one hair from Pattern D
   e) one face from Pattern E
   f) one paper lunch bag
   g) one paper clip
   Clip a–e together on the paper bag with the paper clip.

Procedure: ☆

1. Distribute to each student:
   a) paste
   b) crayons
   c) scissors
   d) puppet packet
   Demonstrate the following steps for the students.
2. Unclip the puppet packet and write your name on the back side of the paper lunch bag. Place the bag aside for now.
3. With black crayon, fill in the letter *A* on the letter card.
4. Cut all duplicated patterns along the dotted lines.
5. With one finger, put paste on the outside edge of the bag *(do not get paste on the flap)*. Place the body on the pasted edge and smooth down.

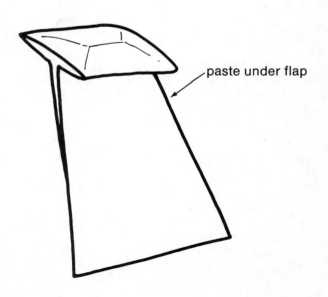

paste under flap

Amy 183

6. Paste the letter card on the body.
7. Put paste on the inside edge of each wing. Place the wings in the creases of the bag, below the flap.

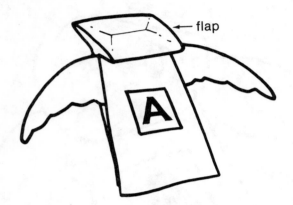

8. Run paste along the straight edge of the face. Place the hair on the pasted edge.
9. With white crayon, draw large ovals for the eyes. Make pupils and lashes with black crayon. Outline the eyes with black crayon. With red crayon, make an oval for the mouth.

10. Paste the halo on top of the hair.

11. Apply paste to the outside edge of the flap. Place the head on the pasted flap and smooth down.
12. Let the puppet dry before using.

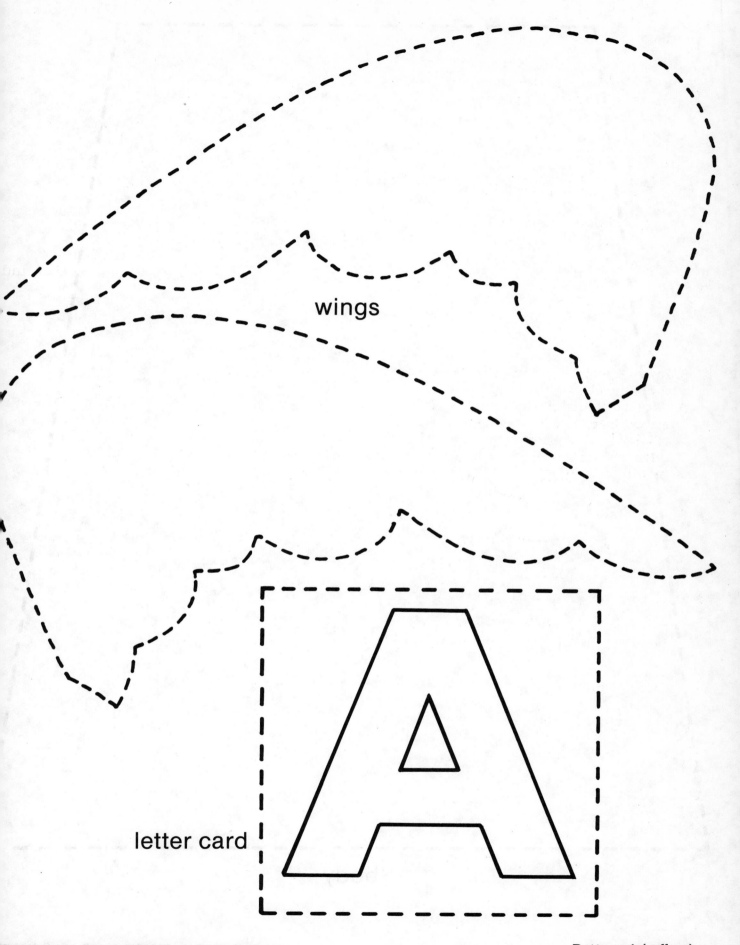

wings

letter card

Pattern A (yellow)

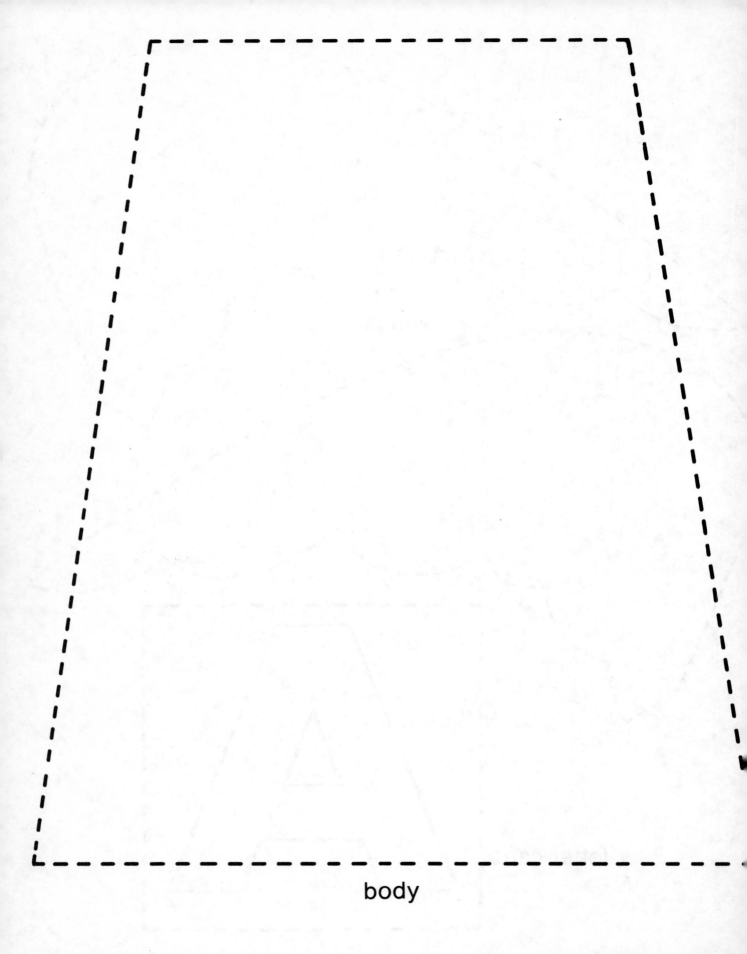

body

Pattern B (pink)

Bagging It with Puppets! © 1988 David S. Lake Publishers

186 Amy

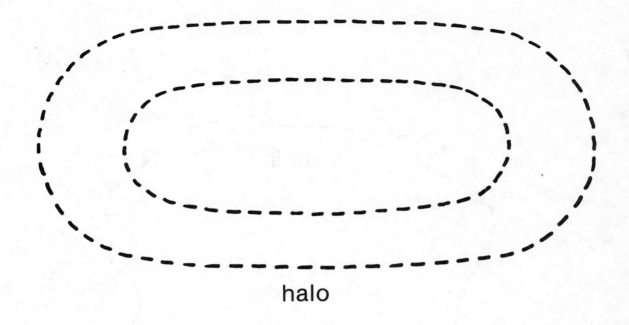

halo

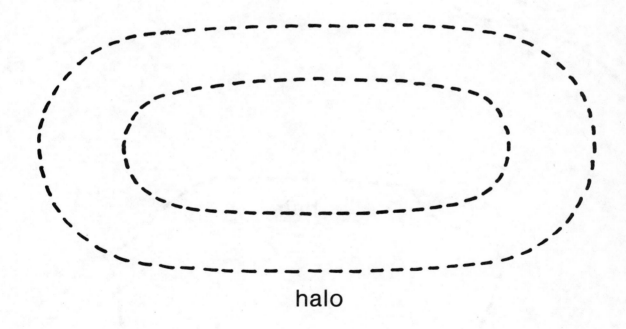

halo

Pattern C (white)

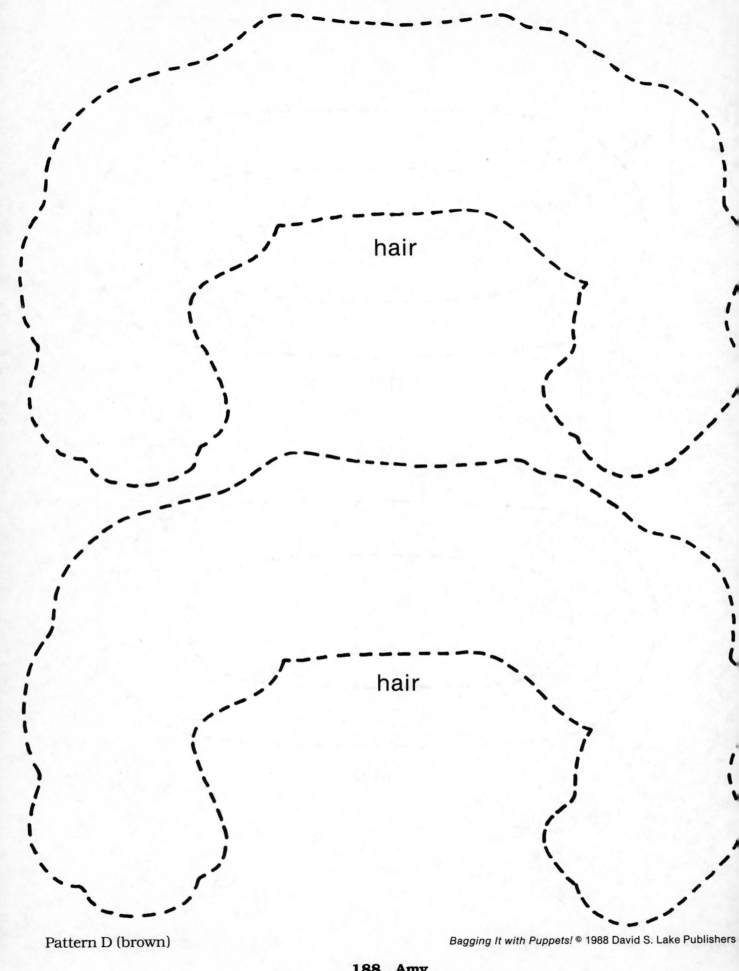

hair

hair

Pattern D (brown)

188 Amy

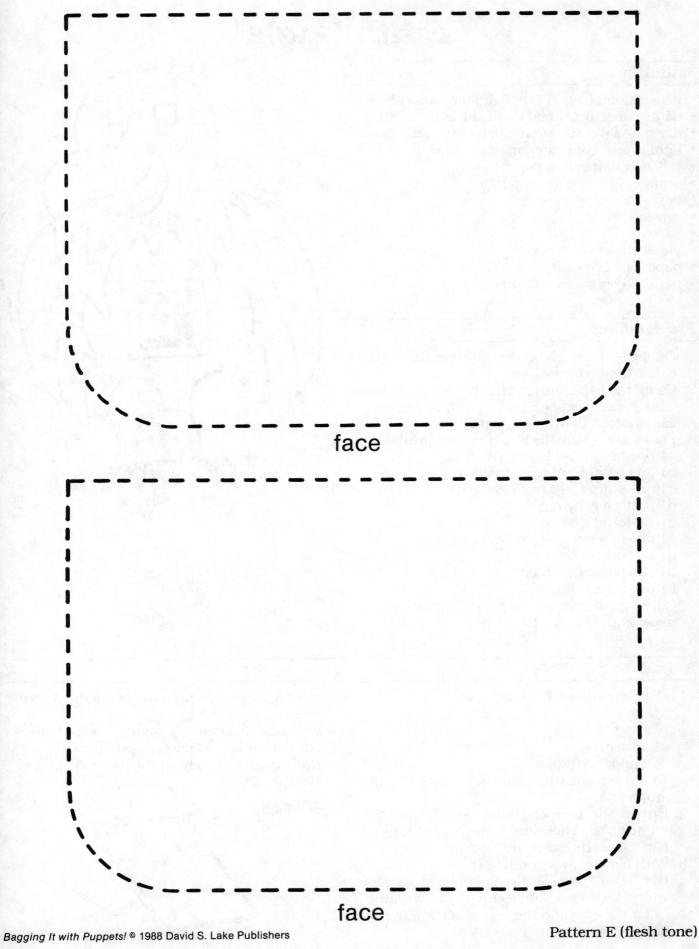

face

face

Pattern E (flesh tone)

Amy 189

Edith Eagle

Materials: ☆

- paper lunch bags (11″ × 5¾″) for puppet base
- white construction paper (head, letter card)
- dark brown construction paper (wings, legs)
- light brown construction paper (body)
- yellow construction paper (beak)
- orange construction paper (feet)
- crayons
- scissors
- paste
- paper clips
- paper cutter
- patterns on pages 192–197

Preparation: ☆

1. Duplicate patterns on the appropriate colored construction paper.
2. Using the paper cutter, cut sheets of light brown construction paper 6″ × 9″ for the body. You can cut four to five sheets at a time.
3. For each child, make a packet containing:
   a) one beak from Pattern A
   b) one pair of feet from Pattern B
   c) one pair of legs from Pattern C
   d) Pattern D (wings)
   e) Pattern E (head)
   f) one letter card from Pattern F
   g) one precut body
   h) one paper lunch bag
   i) one paper clip
   Clip a–g together on the paper bag with the paper clip.

Procedure: ☆

1. Distribute to each student:
   a) paste
   b) crayons
   c) scissors
   d) puppet packet
   Demonstrate the following steps for the students.
2. Unclip the puppet packet and write your name on the back side of the paper lunch bag. Place the bag aside for now.
3. With black crayon, outline the letter *E* on the letter card. Outline the head, pupils, wings, beak, legs, and feet with black crayon.
4. Color the eyes and the inside of the letter *E* with yellow crayon.
5. Cut all duplicated patterns along the dotted lines.
6. With one finger, apply paste to the outside edge of the bag (*do not get paste on the flap*). Place the body on the pasted edge and smooth down.

paste under flap

7. Apply paste to the outside edge of the flap. Place the head on the pasted flap and smooth down.

8. Apply paste to the back of the beak and attach it to the head.

beak

9. Run paste along the back of each wing. Use the neck as a guide to place the wings on the body.

10. Paste the legs to the bottom of the bag. Paste the feet under the legs.

11. Paste the letter *E* on the body, below the neck.

12. Let the puppet dry before using.

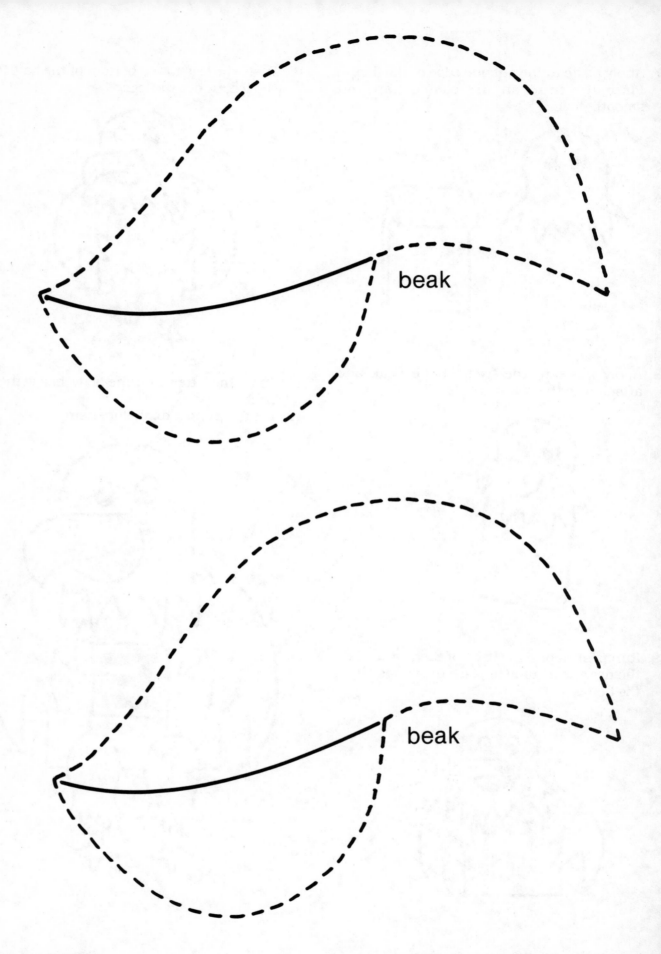

beak

beak

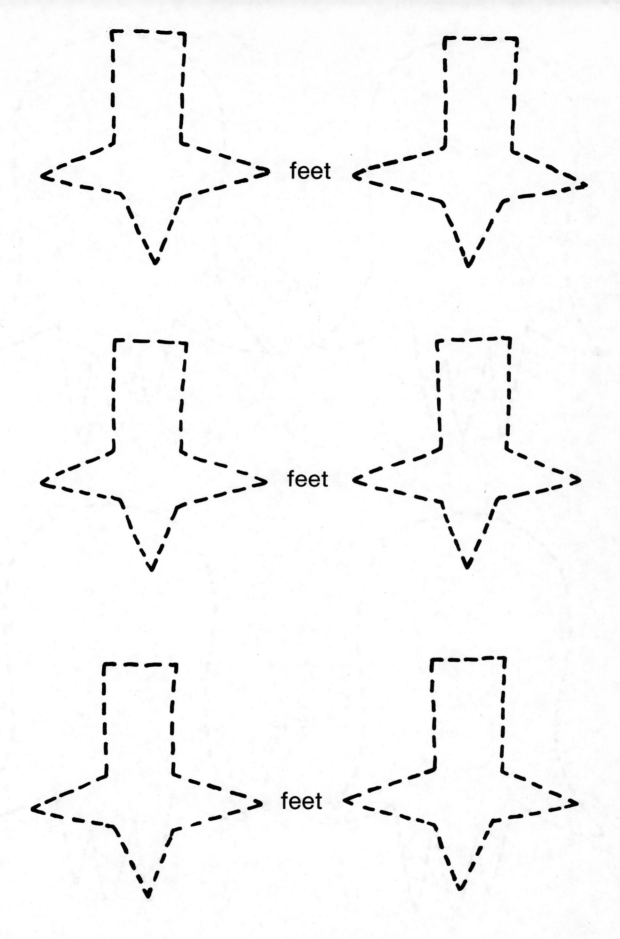

feet

feet

feet

Pattern B (orange)

Eagle   193

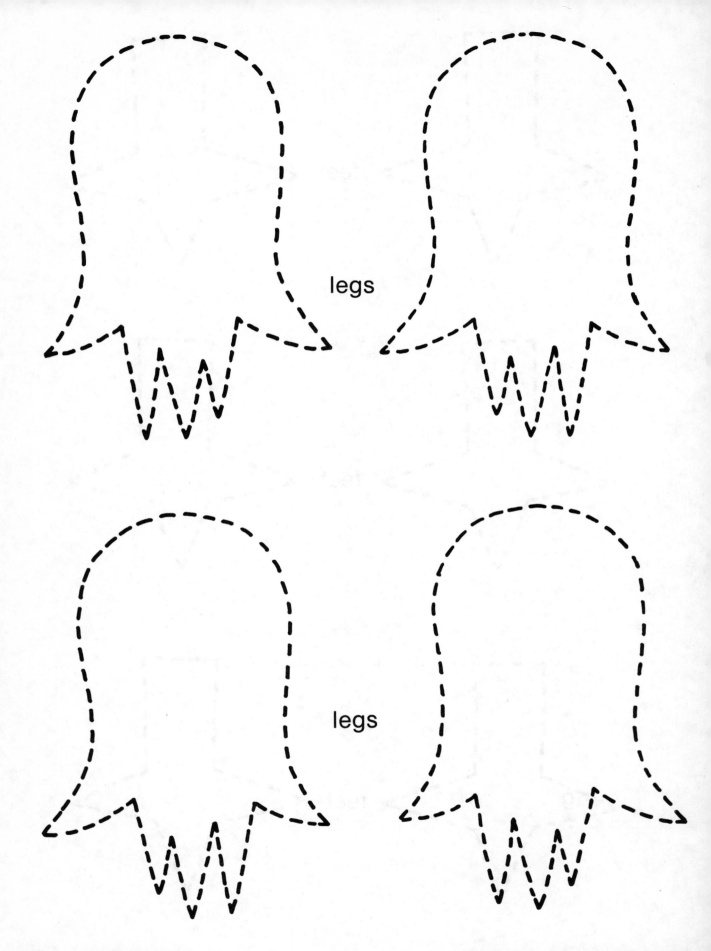

legs

legs

Pattern C (dark brown)

Bagging It with Puppets! © 1988 David S. Lake Publishers

wing

wing

Pattern D (dark brown)

Eagle 195

head

Bagging It with Puppets! © 1988 David S. Lake Publishers

letter card

letter card

letter card

letter card

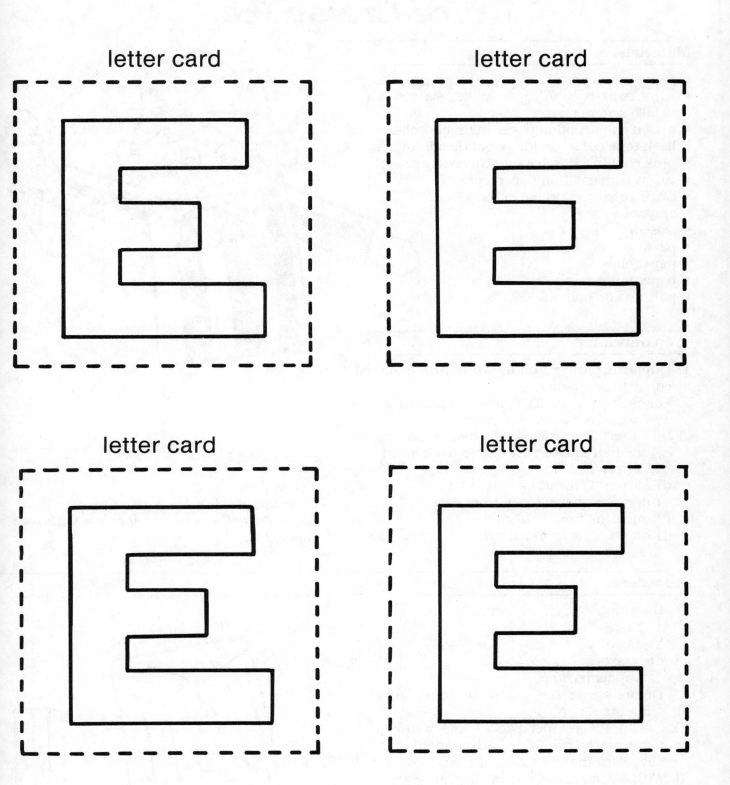

Pattern F (white)

Ice-Cream Ike

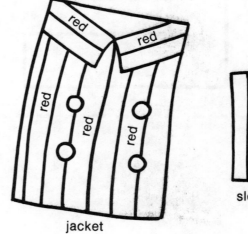

Materials: ☆

- paper lunch bags (11″ × 5¾″) for puppet base
- white construction paper (jacket, sleeves, hat, vanilla scoop)
- brown construction paper (hair, chocolate scoop)
- flesh tone construction paper (head, ears, hands)
- pink construction paper (strawberry scoop)
- yellow construction paper (cone)
- black construction paper (bow tie)
- crayons
- scissors
- paste
- paper clips
- paper cutter
- patterns on pages 200–206

Preparation: ☆

1. Duplicate patterns on the appropriate colored construction paper.
2. For each child, make a packet containing:
   a) Pattern A (jacket, one sleeve)
   b) Pattern B (vanilla scoop, hat, one sleeve)
   c) one hair and one chocolate scoop from Pattern C
   d) Pattern D (head, ears, hands)
   e) one strawberry scoop from Pattern E
   f) one cone from Pattern F
   g) one bow tie from Pattern G
   h) one paper lunch bag
   i) one paper clip
   Clip a–g together on the paper bag with the paper clip.

Procedure: ☆

1. Distribute to each student:
   a) paste
   b) crayons
   c) scissors
   d) puppet packet
   Demonstrate the following steps for the students.
2. Unclip the puppet packet and write your name on the back side of the paper lunch bag. Place the bag aside for now.
3. With black crayon, outline the inner lines of the jacket, hat, and buttons.
4. Color the middle stripe on each sleeve red.
5. Color the top stripe on the collar red.
6. Color the three stripes on the jacket red.

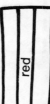

jacket

sleeve

7. Color the letter *I* on the hat red.
8. Color the jacket buttons gold.
9. Cut all duplicated patterns along the dotted lines.
10. With one finger, put paste on the outside edge of the bag *(do not get paste on the flap)*. Place the jacket on the pasted edge and smooth down.

paste below flap →

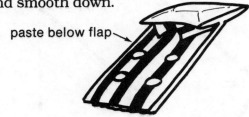

11. Run paste on the inside edge of each sleeve. Attach the sleeves below the flap, in the creases of the bag. Paste the bow tie on the collar.

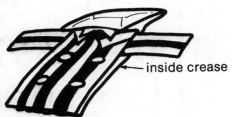

← inside crease

12. Run paste along the inside edge of each hand. Paste the hands, thumbs up, behind the sleeves.

paste →

13. Run paste along the straight edge of the head. Attach the hair.
14. Apply paste to the top edge of the hair. Place the hat on the hair.

15. Run paste along the straight edge of each ear. Paste the ears below the hat, on the back side of the head.

paste →

16. With crayons, add the facial features. With white crayon, color two large ovals for the eyes. Outline the eyes with black. Add pupils and lashes. Add the nose. With red crayon, add the mouth. Make cheeks with pink crayon.

17. Apply paste to the outside edge of the flap. Place the head on the pasted flap.

paste →

18. With brown crayon, outline the inner lines of the ice-cream cone.
19. Run paste along the top of the cone. Paste on the chocolate scoop. Paste on the strawberry scoop. Paste on the vanilla scoop.

paste →

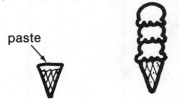

20. Let the puppet dry before using.

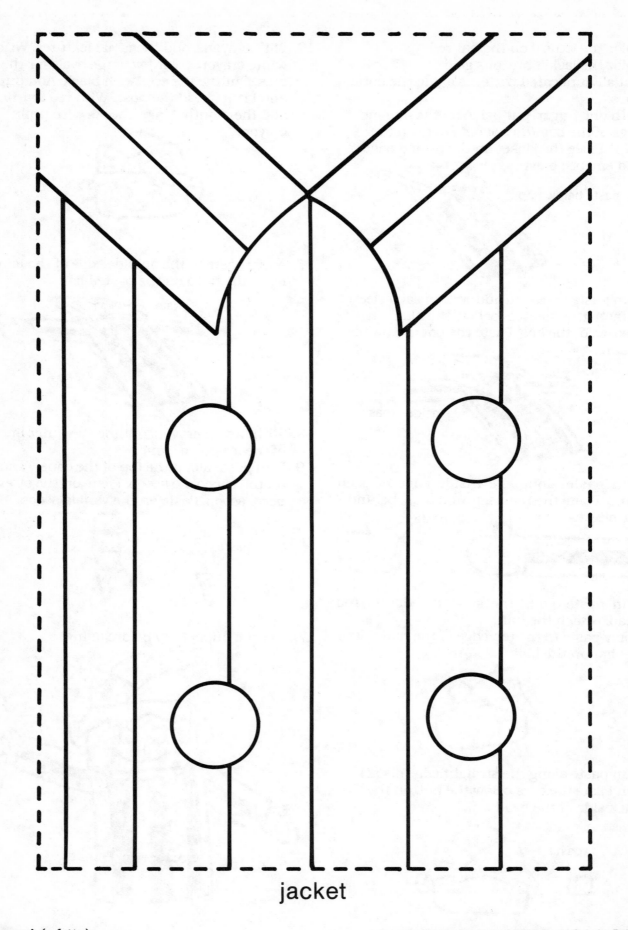

jacket

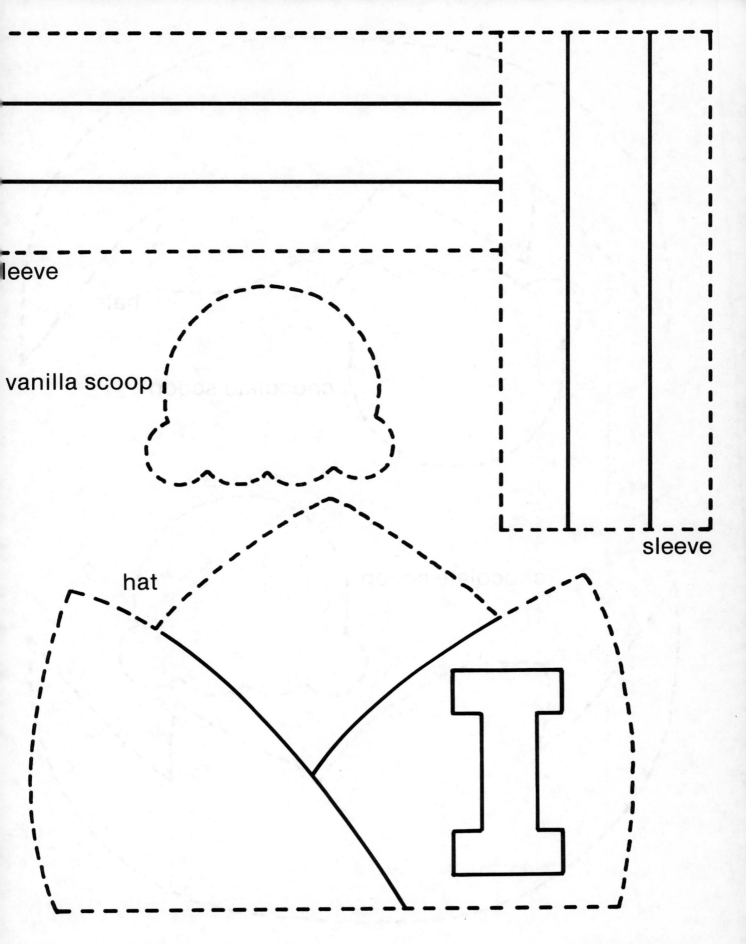

leeve

vanilla scoop

sleeve

hat

I

Pattern B (white)

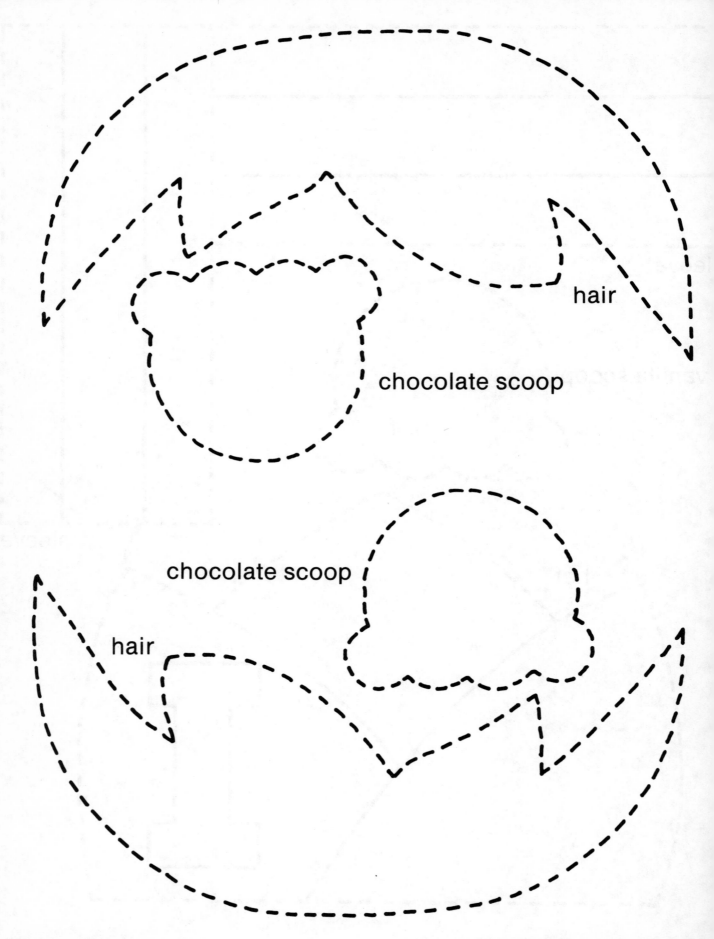

hair

chocolate scoop

chocolate scoop

hair

Pattern C (brown)

Bagging It with Puppets! © 1988 David S. Lake Publishers

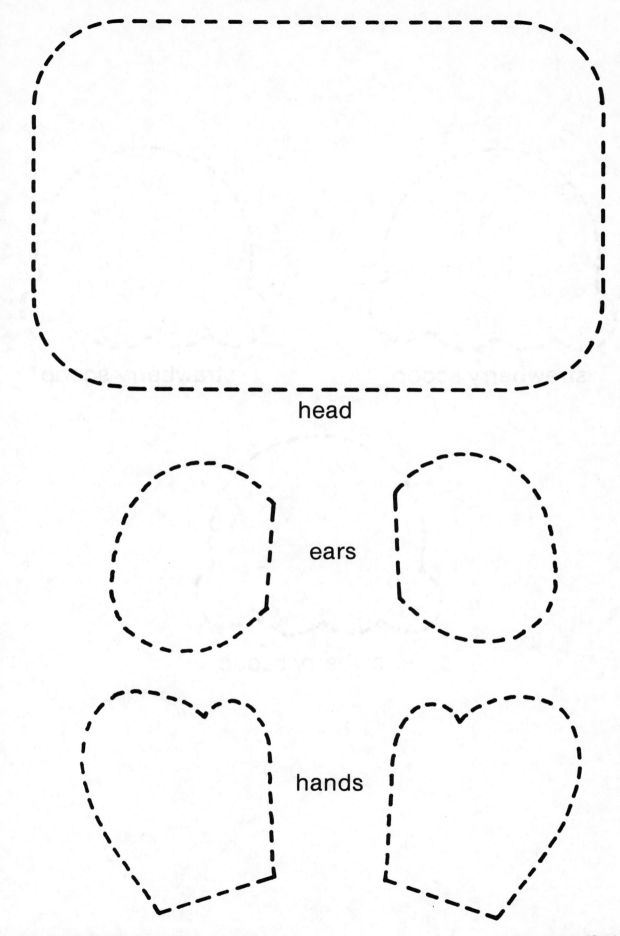

head

ears

hands

Pattern D (flesh tone)

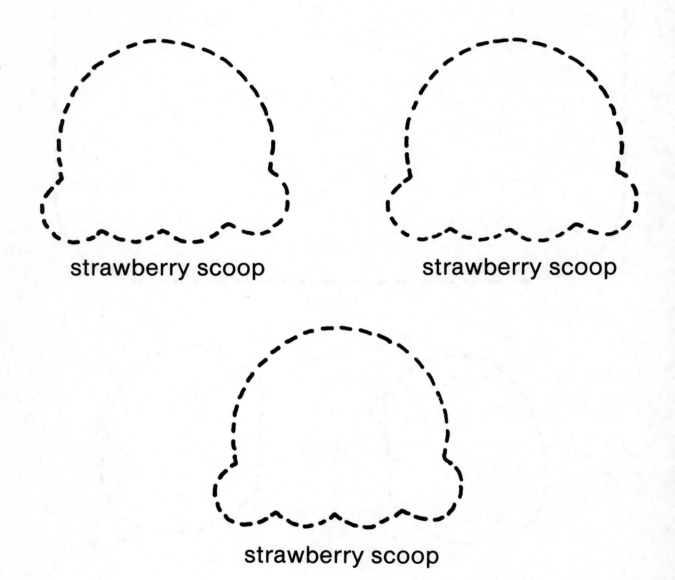

strawberry scoop

strawberry scoop

strawberry scoop

Pattern E (pink)

ice-cream cone   ice-cream cone   ice-cream cone

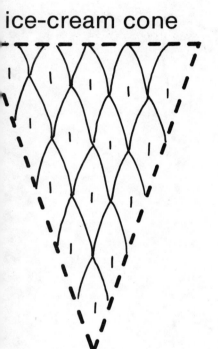
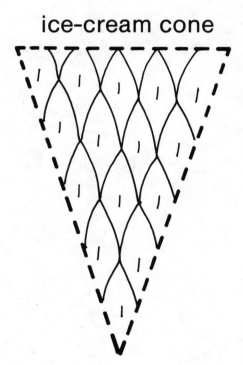
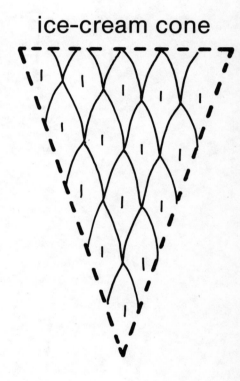

Pattern F (yellow)

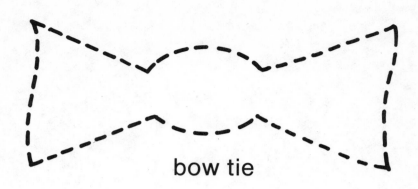

bow tie

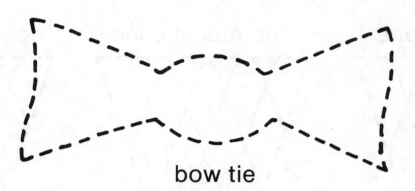

bow tie

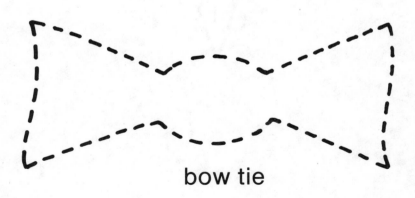

bow tie

Bagging It with Puppets! © 1988 David S. Lake Publishers

Ogie Ogre

Materials: ☆

- paper lunch bags (11″ × 5¾″) for puppet base
- blue-green construction paper (head, arms, legs, letter card)
- brown construction paper (hair, body)
- crayons
- scissors
- paste
- paper clips
- paper cutter
- patterns on pages 209–213

Preparation: ☆

1. Duplicate patterns on the appropriate colored construction paper.
2. For each child, make a packet containing:
   a) Pattern A (body)
   b) Pattern B (hair)
   c) Pattern C (legs, letter card)
   d) Pattern D (arms)
   e) Pattern E (head)
   f) one paper lunch bag
   g) one paper clip
   Clip a–e together on the paper bag with the paper clip.

Procedure: ☆

1. Distribute to each student:
   a) paste
   b) crayons
   c) scissors
   d) puppet packet
   Demonstrate the following steps for the students:
2. Unclip the puppet packet and write your name on the back side of the paper lunch bag. Place the bag aside for now.
3. With black crayon, outline the eyes, nose, mouth, and the letter *O* on the letter card. Color the pupils black.
4. With red crayon, color the tongue.
5. With white crayon, color the eyeballs.
6. Cut all duplicated patterns along the dotted lines.

7. With one finger, put paste on the outside edge of the bag *(do not get paste on the flap)*. Place the body on the pasted edges and smooth down.

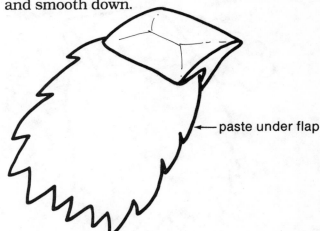

← paste under flap

8. Run paste along the straight edge of the head. Attach the hair.

paste

9. Run paste along the inside edge of each arm. Attach the arms below the flap, in the creases of the bag.

11. Apply paste to the upper edges of the legs. Attach them to the bottom edge of the body. Smooth down.
12. Let the puppet dry before using.

10. Apply paste to the outside edge of the flap. Place the head on the pasted flap and smooth down. Paste the letter card to the body.

paste

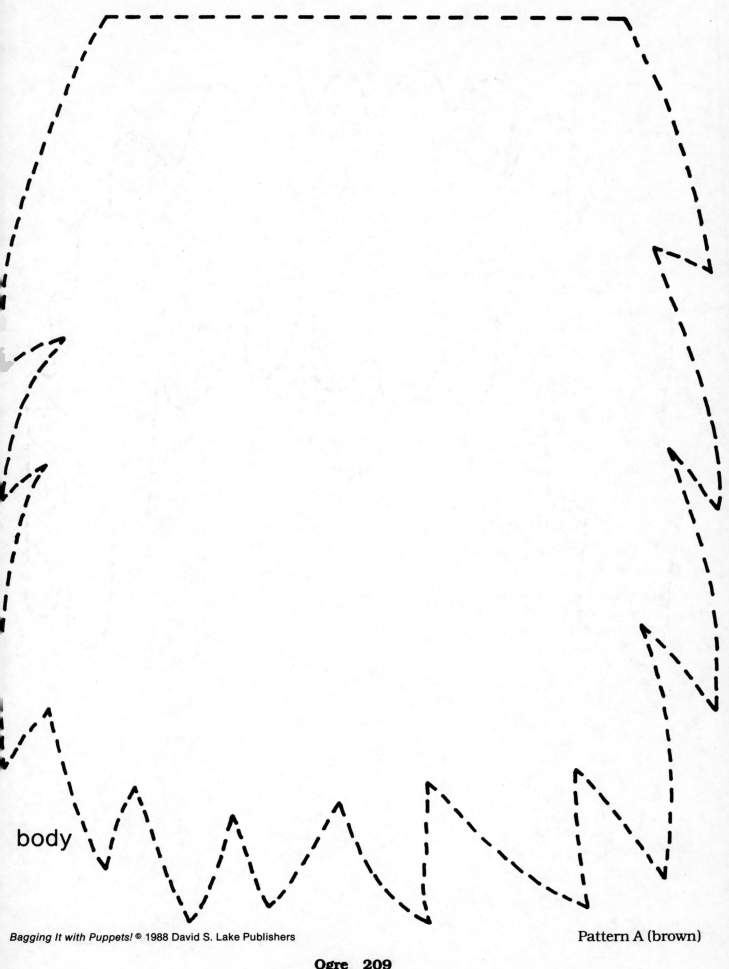

body

Pattern A (brown)

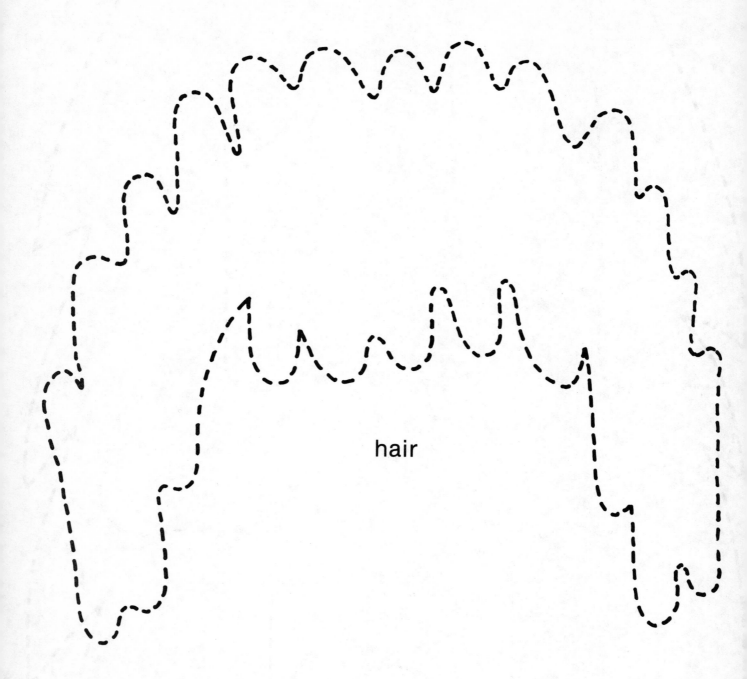

hair

Pattern B (brown)

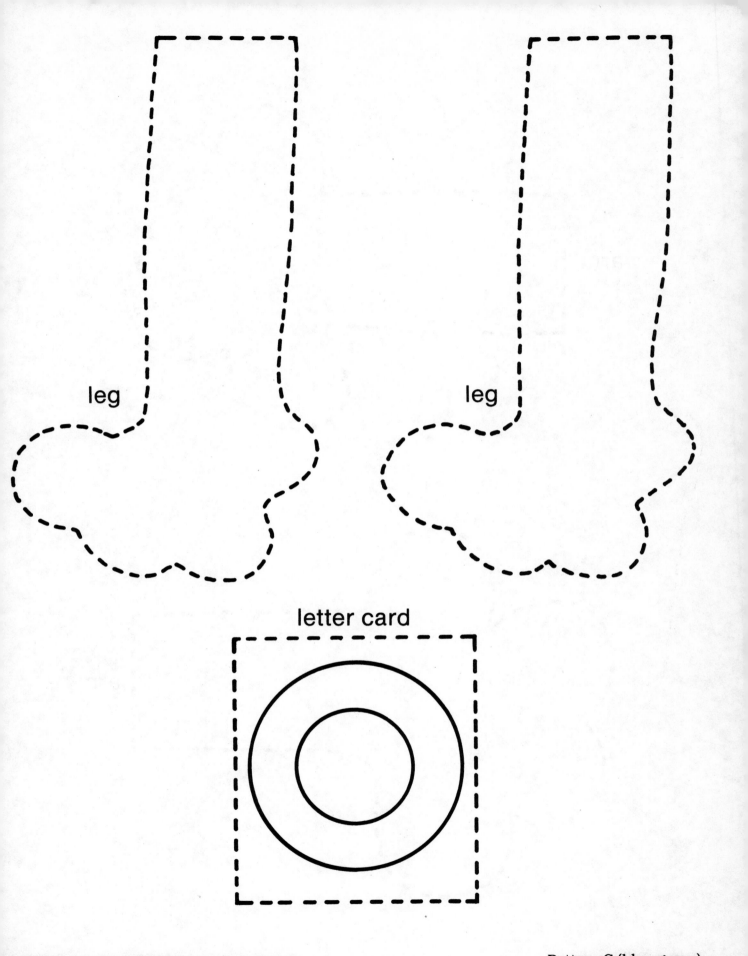

leg

leg

letter card

Pattern C (blue-green)

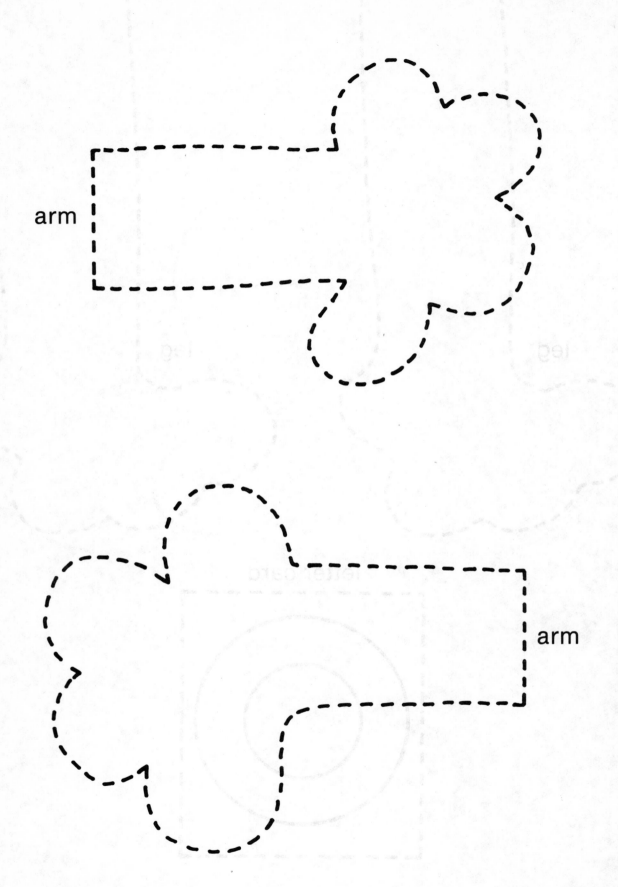

arm

arm

Pattern D (blue-green)

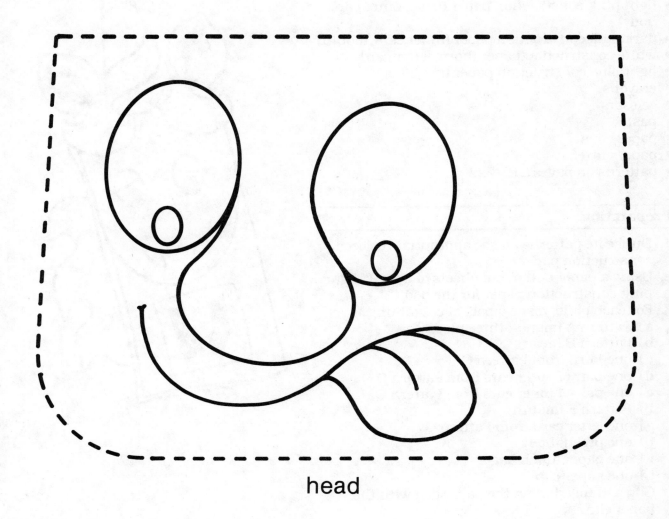

head

Pattern E (blue-green)

Una Unicorn

Materials: ☆

- paper lunch bags (11″ × 5¾″) for puppet base
- light pink construction paper (head, outer ears, body)
- dark pink construction paper (inner ears, mouth)
- white construction paper (horn, letter card)
- light blue construction paper (mane)
- crayons
- scissors
- paste
- paper clips
- paper cutter
- patterns on pages 216–222

Preparation: ☆

1. Duplicate patterns on the appropriate colored construction paper.
2. Using a paper cutter, cut sheets of 6″ × 9″ light pink construction paper for the body.
3. For each child, make a packet containing:
   a) Pattern A (mane—three pieces)
   b) Pattern B (head)
   c) one horn from Pattern C
   d) one pair of outer ears from Pattern D
   e) one pair of inner ears from Pattern E
   f) Pattern F (mouth)
   g) one letter card from Pattern G
   h) one precut body
   i) one paper lunch bag
   j) one paper clip
   Clip a–h together on the paper bag with the paper clip.

Procedure: ☆

1. Distribute to each student:
   a) paste
   b) crayons
   c) scissors
   d) puppet packet
   Demonstrate the following steps for the students.
2. Unclip the puppet packet and write your name on the back side of the paper lunch bag. Place the bag aside for now.
3. With black crayon, fill in the letter *U* on the letter card.
4. Cut all duplicated patterns along the dotted lines.

5. With one finger, put paste on the outside edge of the bag (*do not get paste on the flap*). Place the body on the pasted edge and smooth down.

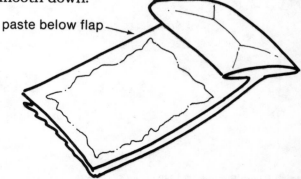

paste below flap

6. Paste the letter card on the body.

7. Apply paste to the inner ears. Place them on the inside of the outer ears.

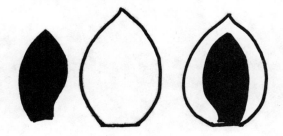

8. Paste the ears on each side of the head.
9. Paste the horn on top of the head, in the center.
10. Paste the two small pieces of the mane on either side of the horn.

11. With white crayon, draw large ovals for the eyes. Outline the eyes with black. Add black lashes and pupils. Outline the nostrils and dots.

12. Apply paste to the outside edge of the flap. Place the head on the pasted flap. Smooth down.

13. Fold mouth along the solid line and paste it below the flap.

14. Paste the large piece of the mane on the side of the body, in the crease of the bag.
15. Let the puppet dry before using.

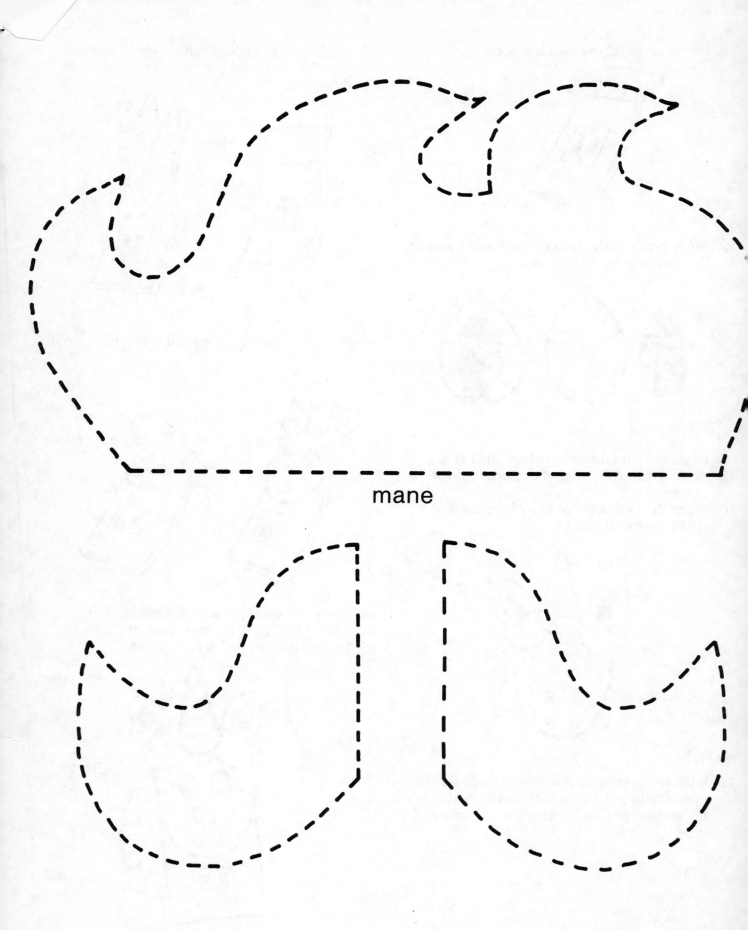

mane

Pattern A (light blue)

Bagging It with Puppets! © 1988 David S. Lake Publishers

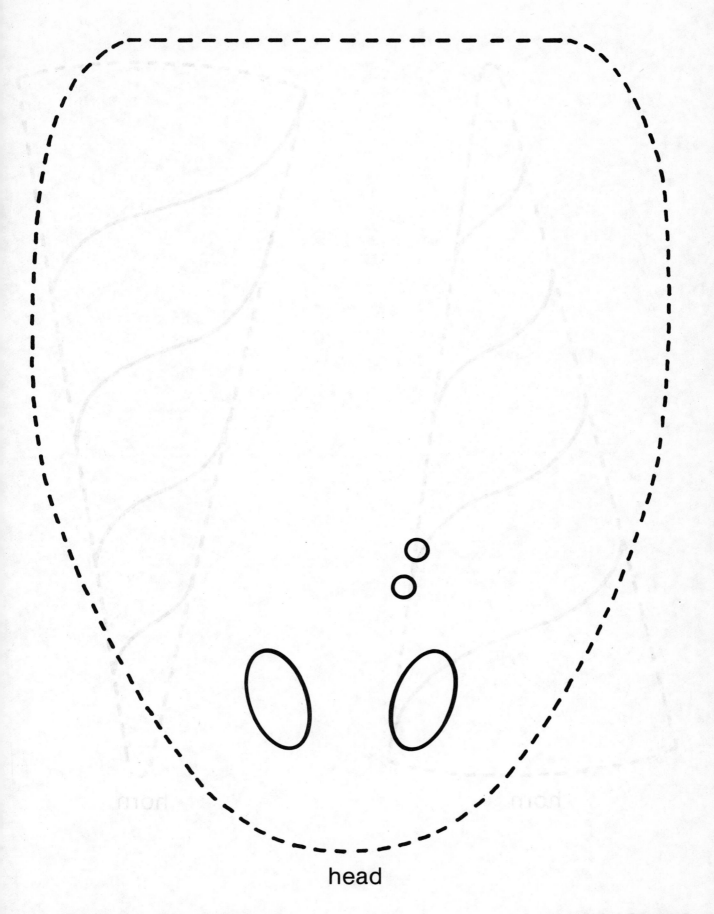

head

Pattern B (light pink)

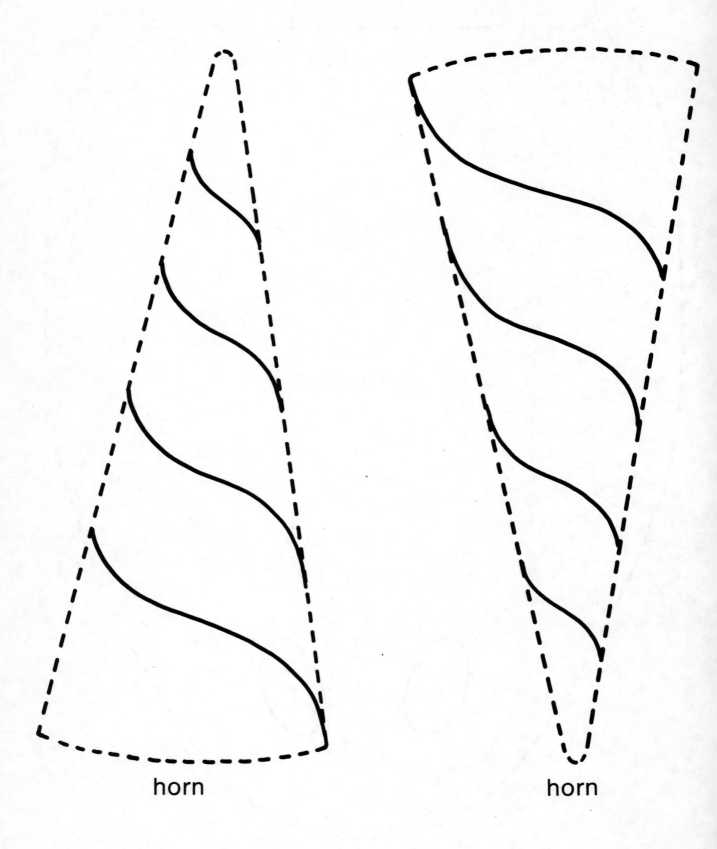

horn

horn

Pattern C (white)

Bagging It with Puppets! © 1988 David S. Lake Publishers

218 Una

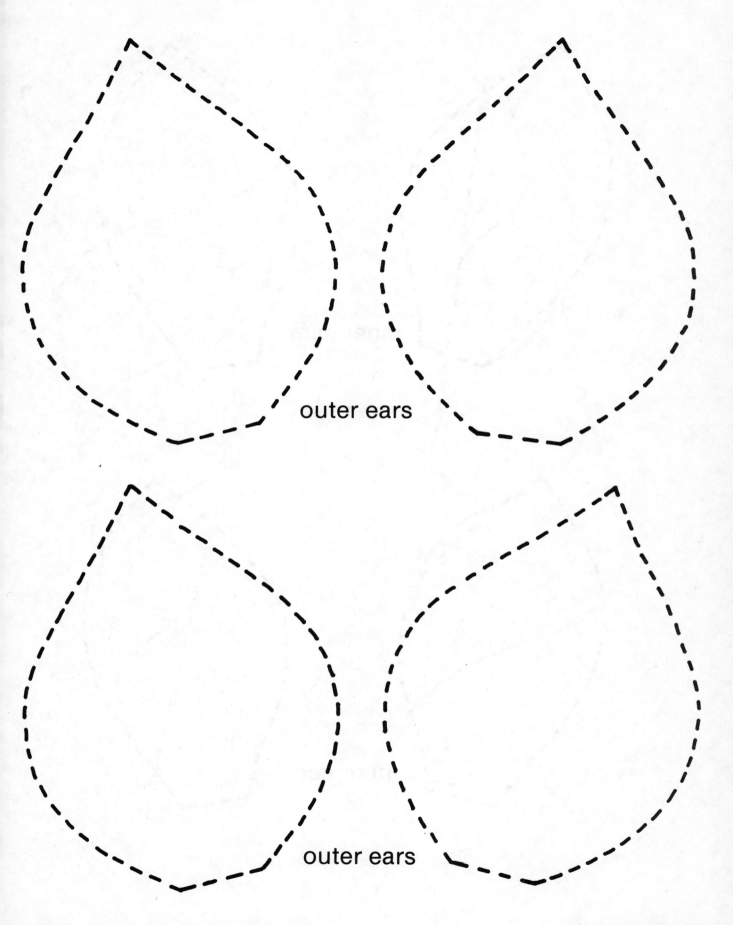

outer ears

outer ears

Pattern D (light pink)

Una 219

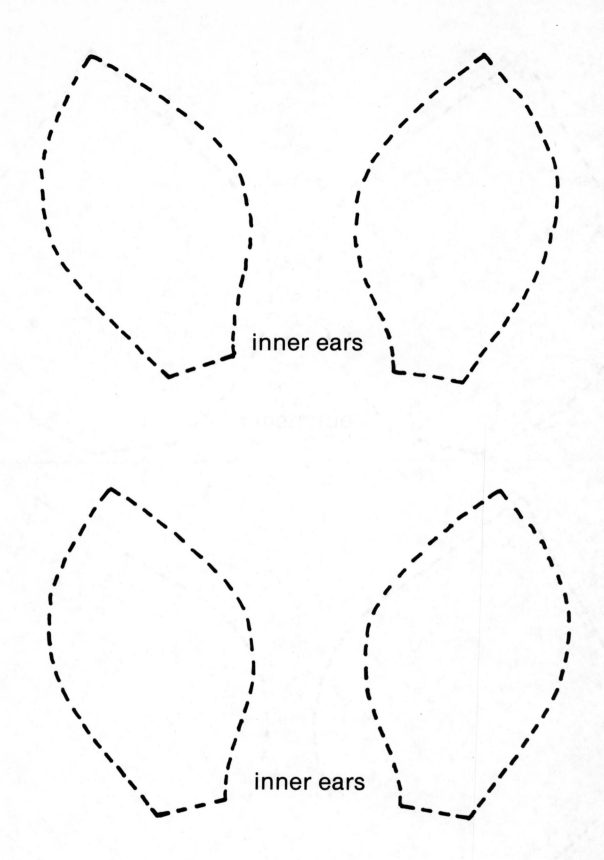

inner ears

inner ears

Pattern E (dark pink)

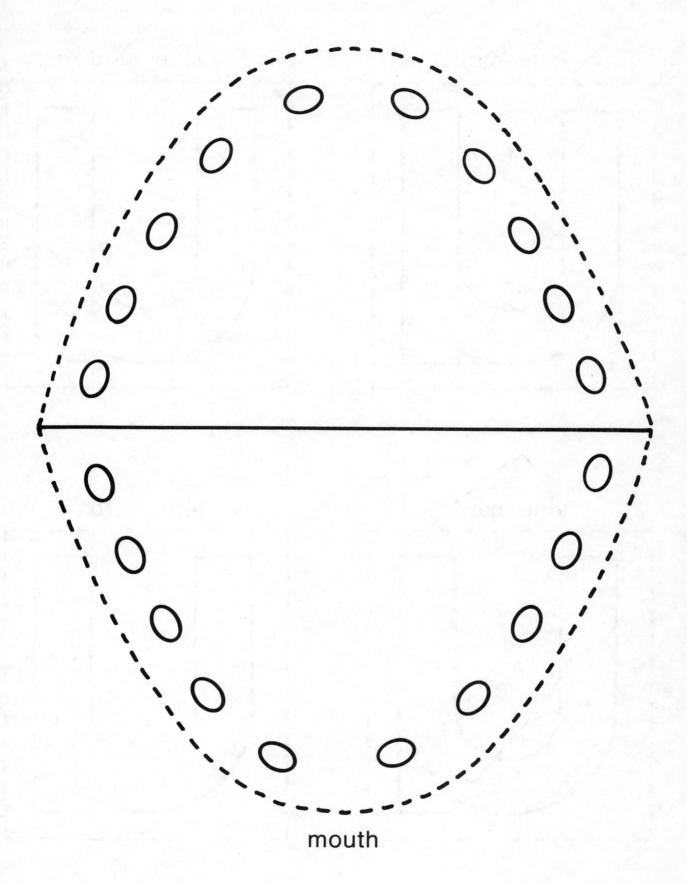

mouth

letter card

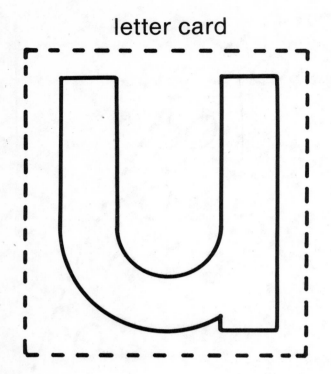

letter card

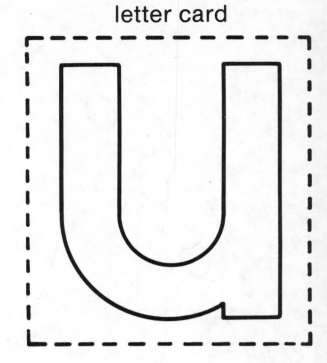

letter card

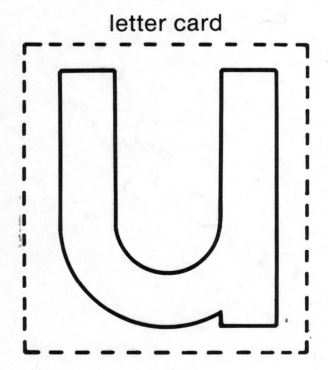

letter card

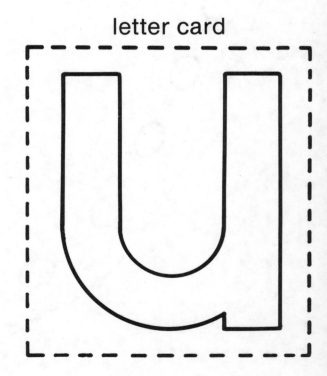

Pattern G (white)

Bagging It with Puppets! © 1988 David S. Lake Publishers